The Way Ahead
Meeting Canada's Productivity Challenge

Governance Series

Governance is the process of effective coordination whereby an organization or a system guides itself when resources, power, and information are widely distributed. Studying governance means probing the pattern of rights and obligations that underpins organizations and social systems; understanding how they coordinate their parallel activities and maintain their coherence; exploring the sources of dysfunction; and suggesting ways to redesign organizations whose governance is in need of repair.

The Series welcomes a range of contributions—from conceptual and theoretical reflections, ethnographic and case studies, and proceedings of conferences and symposia, to works of a very practical nature—that deal with problems or issues on the governance front. The Series publishes works both in French and in English.

The Governance Series is part of the publications division of the Program on Governance and Public Management at the School of Political Studies. Nine volumes have previously been published within this series. The Program on Governance and Public Management also publishes electronic journals: the quarterly www.optimumonline.ca and the biannual www.revuegouvernance.ca

the way ahead

MEETING CANADA'S PRODUCTIVITY CHALLENGE

TOM BRZUSTOWSKI

THE UNIVERSITY OF OTTAWA PRESS
OTTAWA

LIBRARY AND ARCHIVES CANADA CATALOGUING IN PUBLICATION

Brzustowski, T. A. (Thomas A.), 1937-
        The way ahead : meeting Canada's productivity challenge / Tom
Brzustowski.

(Governance series, 1497-2972)
Includes bibliographical references and index.
ISBN 978-0-7766-0669-9

        1. Industrial productivity—Canada.   2. Labor productivity—
Canada.   3. Technological innovations—Economic aspects—Canada.
4. Research, Industrial—Economic aspects—Canada.   5. Canada—
Economic conditions— 21st century.   6. Canada—Economic
policy—21st century.   I. Title.   II. Series: Governance series
(Ottawa, Ont.)

HC120.L3B79 2008   338.060971   C2007-907000-0

Published by the University of Ottawa Press, 2008
542 King Edward Avenue
Ottawa, Ontario K1N 6N5
www.uopress.uottawa.ca

The University of Ottawa Press acknowledges with gratitude
the support extended to its publishing list by Heritage Canada through
its Book Publishing Industry Development Program, by the Canada
Council for the Arts, by the Canadian Federation for the Humanities and
Social Sciences through its Aid to Scholarly Publications Program,
by the Social Sciences and Humanities Research Council,
and by the University of Ottawa.

We also gratefully acknowledge the Telfer School of Management at the
University of Ottawa whose financial support has contributed to the
publication of this book.

Table of Contents

To Fraser Mustard,
for teaching experts to see the big picture

Preface

This is a practical book about economic change. Specifically, it is about the changes that I believe we must make to accelerate our productivity growth and make Canadians' high quality of life sustainable. More particularly still, it describes the important role of science and engineering in meeting the productivity challenge.

Canada is a prosperous country, but it needs to become even more so if we are to maintain our quality of life. Our society is aging, and as the "Baby Boomers" retire and grow older they will not only stop creating wealth in productive work in the economy but will also consume more of society's wealth for their own health care. And whenever we open a newspaper or turn on the TV, we hear about many big and urgent problems beyond health care that already require billions of dollars to solve, and will require even more.

When viewed against this background, our poor record of low productivity growth and the continuing erosion of our purchasing power are a challenge and a warning. Our economy seems a curious mixture of the old and the new. We have a big appetite for the fruits of research and technology available in the modern knowledge-based open global economy, and we import and buy them in large quantities, but our own wealth creation largely depends on economic activity that belongs to an earlier age. We are good at science and engineering, but only a small number of our businesses translate that capability into commercial success. Broadly speaking, we have yet to master using our learning to create prosperity. As a result, we are slowly declining while many other countries are surging ahead. This may seem painless in the short term, but it spells disaster in the long term. Given the financial pressures we already see, we must act now to reverse the productivity trend, and bolster our wealth creation.

The good news is that we have the necessary conditions to do that. Canadians are a civil, peaceful, welcoming and generous society. We attract immigrants, and many among them bring important skills. We have a good education system that includes some world-class universities, excellent research in many important fields of science and engineering, and governments continuing to invest in them. We have very good engineers, strengths in many areas of manufacturing and construction, and we know how to build and manage engineering gigaprojects.[1] We have some splendid examples of technology companies that have become major global successes. And the country is endowed with massive amounts of widely varied natural resources.

But the bad news is that necessary conditions are not sufficient. We must do much more of those things that we know how to do better than anyone else in the world, and we must do much better in all the areas that have been the mainstay of our economy. I think that the right measure in both cases is the value created by Canadians. I believe that we need nothing less than a national commitment to use all the assets at our disposal to create more value across the entire Canadian economy.

Good news, bad news, and now good news again. Solving those formidable problems will not be a one-shot affair. On the contrary, as we go about solving them, Canadians will be learning a great deal. As a result, we will acquire new capabilities and create new capacities that will be of great use in the future. And, in turn, the solutions will open up myriad opportunities for further advancement. If we keep seizing those opportunities, Canada could be riding the economist's "virtuous cycle" (or the engineer's "positive feedback loop") to a very attractive future.

As I set out to write on this subject, I must confess to having some biases. These are beliefs that I have acquired in a variety of ways. Some are based on facts that have been established by research, and some are compelling conjectures that have so far eluded proof. Some others are elements of conventional wisdom that have gone unquestioned for so long that they now seem obvious, and help me make sense of a complex world. And, of course, like anyone else I have biases that are personal values reflecting who I am.

Here are four biases that bear on the subject of this book. To begin with, I believe that it is only the private sector that creates wealth. The public sector consumes wealth as it plays two different roles. First, it provides a supportive and normative framework for wealth creation by the private sector in various appropriate ways, through laws, regulations, treaties, incentives, etc. And, second, it is a concentrator of resources assembled through the tax system. In this role, it pays for the essential activities of society as a whole, such as education, health care and social assistance, which redistribute those concentrated resources. But it also does the very opposite, focusing those resources when it makes investments in major projects.

Secondly, I believe in the essential importance of striving for excellence in everything that we set out to do. In the simplest terms, excellence is being better than anyone else in whatever activity on the scale that is appropriate to that activity (e.g., individual, team, group, company, sector, country, etc.). Excellence begins with competence gained through learning, and it emerges through competition. I don't believe that there are degrees of excellence; either one is excellent or one is not. If Canadians decide to enter some arena for strategic or other reasons, then we must make every effort to achieve excellence in it—to become the best in the world. And if excellence turns out to be beyond reach, then we should recognize that, admit it, and either invest enough time, effort, and resources to reach the necessary level, or vacate the field and move on to something different. I am offended by the caricature of Canadians as people who always "go for bronze," and would relish washing it away with a flood of examples to the contrary.

My third bias might seem a far cry from a discussion of technological and economic issues. I believe that one of the most important measures that a society can take to provide for its future prosperity and well-being is to invest in the development of its children into competent adults. This must begin with providing appropriate advice and care for expectant mothers, continue with good neonatal care for babies, and move on to high-quality early childhood education that makes children intellectually and socially ready for kindergarten. Elementary school is also very important and, in particular, I believe that children should be introduced to science and mathematics by elementary school teachers who themselves have studied science and mathematics at the university level. Even though I can't provide a number for the ideal return on investment, the benefits of such a strategy seem obvious. Children who become competent adults will be able to assume productive roles and contribute to society. In contrast, those whose development is neglected will not only contribute less, but may need to draw on the resources of society through various programs of assistance and care, and in some cases possibly even through the justice system.

The fourth bias can be put as "First make it, then spend it." This is not some theoretical quarrel with Keynesian economists; it's much more visceral than that. In my years in government service, I have too often seen deficits build up the public debt, and then the cost of servicing that debt squeeze some very important expenditures out of the budget. Two priorities that are particularly vulnerable under such circumstances are investments for the long term and current spending on measures that need to be taken now in order to prevent problems later on. My concern with wealth creation is conditioned by this frustrating experience.

This book deals with what Canadians do in their work, how they add value, and how they create wealth. Most of the time, the unit of analysis is the enterprise. I am well aware that there are differences among regions in many aspects of what enterprises do and how they do it, and that federal and provincial jurisdictions affect their activities, but except for the last part of the final chapter, I leave both the regional and the federal-provincial nuances to those who know more about them than I do. My main points can be made treating Canada as a whole. So when I use phrases such as "Canada should" do something or "Canada needs" something, I refer broadly to any and all possible actors, from the individual worker to the top of the federal government, leaving any more particular reference to be inferred from the situation in question. Likewise, I often say "We" as shorthand for "We Canadians" or "Canada."

I also realize that some ideas in this book might belong in the political realm, but the book is not a partisan statement. Where my ideas agree with a policy or plank in the platform of one or another political party, then we obviously see things the same way. And if an idea in the book specifically opposes some such initiative, nobody should take that as partisan criticism. It simply means that my reasoning has led me to the opposite conclusion; if that proves persuasive, then so much the better. There may also be ideas in this book that could be new and attractive to certain political parties. In that case, they are welcome to adopt them. In fact, I would be delighted if all political parties found ideas in this book that they wanted to make their own.

Much of the material that follows builds on what I have learned from the work of others. In cases where I can trace my learning to a single source, I provide the reference in the traditional way. But I have also learned by listening to wise persons who themselves synthesized the work of many scholars, and created a big picture for others to see. There, I found the referencing more difficult, with one exception. I have learned a great deal from Dr. J. Fraser Mustard, the founding president of the Canadian Institute for Advanced Research (CIFAR), and a leading thinker about today's most important social and economic issues, and their interplay. Mustard is a visionary who can scan the landscape of research results in many different fields and distil from it what he calls "a framework of understanding." My thinking and learning owes much to Fraser Mustard, particularly in the role he played through the late 1980s and early 1990s on the Ontario Premier's Council, and it is for that reason that I dedicate this book to him.

Preface

Finally, let me express my appreciation to the Telfer School of Management and to the University of Ottawa, and particularly to Dean Micheal Kelly and President Gilles Patry for giving me the opportunity to reinvent myself as a management professor, eighteen years after I left the university world as a professor of mechanical engineering. The appointment at the Telfer school has given me the time to pursue in depth some of the subjects to which my eyes had been opened during my years in the provincial and federal public service, namely innovation, commercialization, and wealth creation. It also gave me the invaluable company of new colleagues and students with whom, and from whom, to learn more.

I also want to express my appreciation to the Royal Bank of Canada Financial Group for sponsoring the Professorship in the Commercialization of Innovations to which I have been appointed. I think it is very important that the country's largest financial institution should so visibly associate itself with an area that is crucial to Canada's economic future, and yet remains largely invisible to the public. As thousands of students pass through the Telfer School of Management, I am sure that this far-sighted gesture by RBC will prove of strategic value, by showing them that innovation and commercialization are vital elements of the economic environment in which they will be making their contributions.

Last and most important, I wish to express my wholehearted gratitude to my wife Louise. Her patient support of my work was essential during the writing of this book, just as it has been for all the accomplishments of my working life.

Tom Brzustowski
Ottawa, November 2007

NOTE:

1 Megaprojects are no longer impressive; you don't get much of a project for a few million ("mega") dollars these days. Today's big ones cost billions—hence "giga."

Introduction

This book is written to inform and to motivate, as a prod to change. It connects the dots, showing that education, skills, knowledge, R&D, value-added, wealth creation, productivity, innovation, entrepreneurship, commercialization, competitiveness, global trade, and many related issues are all part of the same big picture, the picture of Canada's future prosperity in the making today. It is written for members of the general public who care about our economic future and our quality of life, as well as decision makers in the private and public sectors. This book is not an academic treatise, but its endnotes contain some explanations of complex items and references to the sources of information used.

The subtitle of the book refers to Canada's productivity challenge because the sustainability of our prosperity is intimately tied up with growing productivity. The demographics of Canada's population make increasing our productivity growth imperative. But the productivity challenge can be met. We know what must be done; it really isn't rocket science. Instead, it is just a matter of developing the right national strategy and getting our acts together—many acts. But that needs strong leadership to guide us through the necessary qualitative change.

The Way Ahead

For starters, we must be persuaded to abandon two misconceptions that are holding us back. First, there is the idea that a silver bullet might be found, some single brilliant initiative that will catapult us into the secure economic position that is our deserved destiny, and all we need to do is wait for somebody to come up with it. And, second, I think we suffer from a widely held but seldom voiced complacency, the belief that our enormous reservoir of natural riches will always be there to take care of our needs. There will always be a big pie on the table, and our main concern is to divide the pie fairly.

Canada is a very prosperous country, and to a large degree it has been our rich endowment of natural resources that has gotten us here; but now our prosperity needs to grow even greater and become sustainable if we are to maintain our high quality of life in the face of growing pressures.

Demographics provide the most obvious and unavoidable pressure. Our population is steadily growing older, with two effects that add up to a major challenge. First, the aging population needs more and more health care as we live longer and must manage chronic diseases for a longer time. Second, the workforce that provides the resources to pay for that health care will decline in proportion to the population as the baby-boom generation retires. And in addition to health care and the issues of an aging society, we must deal with many other increasingly urgent problems that require large current expenditures, massive capital investments, or both. I mean child poverty, homelessness, and the unacceptably low standard of living of many Aboriginal people. I mean a great range of energy, climate-change and environmental issues, specifically including urban waste management. I mean inadequate, obsolete, or decaying physical infrastructure of all sorts, with too many bottlenecks in the transportation of goods. I mean the need to play a meaningful role in helping the developing world to improve the lives of millions of people. And I also mean the growing challenges of maintaining our own sovereignty in the increasingly accessible waters of the Arctic. Solving these and other important problems will require the investment of both public and private wealth on a massive scale and for a long time. And to create the capacity to meet these financial pressures, we must both increase our prosperity and make it sustainable.

Unfortunately, our capacity to create the wealth to pay for solving these problems is not what it should be. Our educational system itself needs major investments so that Canadians might keep up in skills and knowledge with our competitors, and so that Aboriginal youth might have the same prospects for success as all other young people. Our natural resources are still plentiful, but we rely excessively on the export of raw materials. As a result, Canadian producers are hostage to swings in world commodity prices and, in the long term, competition from poorer countries is driving those prices down. Canadians are very good in many areas of manufacturing, but we make too many commodity products, our productivity has been growing too slowly, and our competitiveness has depended for too long on a low dollar. And even when the dollar is high and companies have cash on hand, investments in worker training, and in imported machinery and equipment to raise productivity have been lagging.

Our scientific research has become very strong, but we have still to master using new knowledge to create new wealth. We have very strong engineering education in modern fields and some great technology companies selling to the world, but there are too few of them, and we still import more than we export in high-tech products. We are a trading nation, more dependent on trading than almost any other, but we haven't taken advantage of our multicultural society to develop into a world marketing powerhouse. We also seem to have developed the disquieting reputation of being slow to seize economic opportunities that present themselves, even when they are of our own making. The challenge is to assemble our advantages, muster our strengths, and start to use them strategically and effectively to increase Canada's prosperity and make it sustainable at the higher level.

The nine chapters of this book present a strategy for doing that. In the starkest terms, the strategy is to shift Canada from a commodity economy to an innovation economy. That means moving from an excessive dependence on raw materials and undifferentiated products across many sectors to much greater reliance on value-added differentiated products and Canadian innovations across all sectors, taking advantage of our strengths in science and engineering. This change must be made both by revising what is done in existing industries and by creating new ventures to exploit new technologies. And it can't be a short ride up to the next plateau where we can sit back and relish our achievements; it has to be a continuous climb up the down escalator.

Such deep change will not be accomplished by a single act of heroic leadership. On the contrary, what is needed is a sustained, concerted effort by many players on many fronts, building on initiatives that have worked for many enterprising Canadians, removing the internal obstacles to our progress that have already been identified many times, using Canadian markets as the proving ground for our exports, and adapting promising ideas from successful strategies around the world.

The responsibility for succeeding falls mainly on the private sector, but business cannot succeed unless Canada's governments at all levels provide consistent, predictable, and appropriate supporting frameworks. That requires wise public policy, prompt and effective decision making, consistent and transparent procedures, appropriate procurement practices, as well as effective administration of proper incentives and controls. In general terms, laws and regulations must be treated as instruments more for enabling and channeling than for inhibiting. And to connect those frameworks with the people who actually do the work and create the wealth, public service of high quality must be delivered effectively by dedicated people. Against that background, our public institutions must maintain their valuable arm's-length independence from the vested interests of the day and keep an eye on the long term. Effective leadership will be essential in this process, but it will have to be the leadership of many.

Canada in the World

In some ways a giant...

W hat are Canada's economic prospects in the world of the twenty-first century? To answer this question, this chapter presents a comparison between Canada and the other twenty-two most important economies, using a selection of readily available data. These data were chosen for their relevance to the issues that will shape the country's future. The chapter then moves on to examine a recent correlation of prosperity with excellence in science and engineering that is relevant to the knowledge-based global economy in which Canada's prospects must be realized.

How Canada compares with the top economies

Canada is the second-largest country in the world, larger than the United States or China by an area about the size of Germany. Only Russia is larger.

Among the 23 top industrialized countries, Canada is the fifth most prosperous, and has the 13th largest population and the 11th largest economy.[1] Table 1.1 lists four important characteristics for 23 of the world's most industrialized nations. Three are economic: the gross domestic product (GDP) in so-called purchasing power parity[2] (PPP) dollars for the year 2005,[3] the population in the same year, and the GDP per capita for 2005. That last quantity will be referred to as "prosperity."[4] The fourth key characteristic is geographic: the area of the country, included to give some indication of its size. The table also includes the average (GDP per capita) for the world, a far less accurate number than those for the group of 23. Nevertheless, this rough value serves to show that Canadian prosperity is about three and a half times the world average.

The numbers in Table 1.1 clearly show that the traditional "ten times larger" ratio of the US to Canada is only a rough approximation. The US population is 9.0 times larger, and the US economy is 11.5 times larger. The fact that the ratio of economies is larger than the ratio of populations is another indicator of the productivity gap that we need to close.

Table 1.2 shows how Canada ranks among the 23 in a number of selected dimensions. The full set of data from which these comparisons were extracted can be found in the appendix.

Canada's population density is the second lowest in the group, 33 times smaller than the median value, and 200 times smaller than Taiwan's. Only Australia's is less. But that is really only part of the story. The recent census[5] has shown that 80% of Canadians live in cities. That means that over most of our land the population density is even lower, by a factor near five.[6] Such a low population density over a vast area has very significant implications for the communications and transportation infrastructure required to sustain small remote communities. The high cost of that infrastructure is part of the "operating cost" of Canada.

TABLE 1.1   A gross comparison of 23 industrialized nations

	GDP (2005 PPP) $ trillion	pop. (2005)	area, sq.km.	GDP/cap (2005 PPP) $
US	12.37	295,734,000	9,631,418	41,800
China	8.158	1,306,314,000	9,596,960	6,200
Japan	3.867	127,417,000	377,835	30,400
India	3.678	1,080,264,000	3,287,590	3,400
Germany	2.446	82,431,000	357,021	29,700
UK	1.867	60,441,000	244,820	30,900
France	1.816	60,656,000	547,030	29,900
Italy	1.645	58,103,000	301,230	28,300
Brazil	1.58	186,113,000	8,511,965	8,500
Russia	1.535	143,420,000	17,075,200	10,700
Canada	1.077	32,805,000	9,984,670	32,800
Mexico	1.066	106,203,000	1,972,550	10,000
Spain	1.014	40,341,000	504,782	25,100
S. Korea	0.9833	48,423,000	98,480	20,300
Australia	0.6427	20,090,000	7,686,850	32,000
Taiwan	0.6108	22,894,000	35,980	26,700
Netherlands	0.500	16,407,000	41,526	30,500
Sweden	0.2665	9,002,000	449,964	29,600
Switzerland	0.2621	7,489,000	41,290	35,000
Norway	0.1947	4,593,000	324,220	42,400
Finland	0.1584	5,223,000	338,145	30,300
Israel	0.1392	6,277,000	20,770	22,200
Ireland	0.1369	4,016,000	70,280	34,100
WORLD				**9,300**

TABLE 1.2   How Canada ranks according to some important
parameters

measure	3 highest		median value	3 lowest		Canada
Population density, persons/sq.km.	Taiwan South Korea Netherlands	636 492 395	111	Australia Canada Russia	2.61 3.29 8.40	3.29
Median age	Japan Germany Italy	42.64 42.16 41.77	38.17	India Mexico Brazil	24.66 24.93 27.81	38.54
Ratio of the labour force to population	China Canada Germany	0.606 0.529 0.526	0.500	Mexico Israel Italy	0.352 0.386 0.421	0.529
Arable land loading, pers./sq.km.	Taiwan South Korea Japan	2960 2870 2790	520	Australia Canada Russia	40 73 115	73
Industry share of GDP, %	China Ireland South Korea	53.1 46.0 41.4	28.7	Brazil US France	14.0 20.7 21.4	29.1
Services share of GDP, %	US France Japan and Netherlands	78.3 76.1 73.5	67.9	China Ireland India	32.5 49.0 51.4	68.7
Annual electricity consumption per capita, kWh/cap.yr.	Canada Finland Sweden	15880 15110 14641	6264	India China Mexico	480.0 1661 1826	15880
Per capita daily oil consumption, bbl/cap.day	US Canada Netherlands Norway	0.0677 0.0668 0.0561 0.0560	0.0384	India China Brazil	0.0021 0.0049 0.0113	0.0668
Telephone land lines per capita, no./cap.	Sweden Norway Switzerland	0.731 0.727 0.724	0.538	India Mexico China	0.045 0.150 0.201	0.608
Land lines plus mobiles per capita, no./cap.	Taiwan Norway Sweden	1.679 1.633 1.614	1.335	India China Mexico	0.069 0.407 0.415	1.011

Canada is in the mainstream of the "23" by most measures, except for four of those shown in Table 1.2. Canada is at the high end in the ratio of labour force to population, and in the consumption of electrical energy and oil. It is at the low end in population density and population per unit area of arable land.

Table 1.2 does not compare coastlines, but Canada has by far the longest coastline in the world, more than five times longer than Russia's and almost seven times longer than Japan's. On paper, that makes us potentially the leading maritime nation, with huge benefits from off-shore resources and ocean access to the world. In practice, much of our coastline is in the north and the far north, where the challenges are as enormous as the assets.

The median age of Canada's population is only slightly greater than the median age for the 23, and its age structure is not very different from the median structure. But our population is significantly older than those of our NAFTA partners. Mexicans have a median age of 24.93, and Americans 36.27, compared with Canadians' 38.54. In Canada, 17.9% of the population is younger than 14. In the US and Mexico, those numbers are 20.6 and 31.1%, respectively. And at the other end of the scale, 13.2% of Canadians are 65 or older, compared with 12.4% of Americans and only 5.6% of Mexicans. Demographics have major implications for the economy, and we will be revisiting them in a later chapter.

The number of people per square kilometre of arable land—call it arable land loading—is a measure of the ability of a country's agriculture to feed its people. Low values identify the bread baskets of the world, high values the food importers. Canada is a bread basket.

The composition of the GDP reflects the maturity of the economy. Table 1.2 shows that the younger economies depend much more on industry than on services; the opposite is true in the older ones. At first sight, Brazil seems to be an anomaly, but its situation becomes clearer when agriculture (extraordinarily high at 20%) and industry are considered together, leaving 66% of GDP dependent on services. This number is below the median for the group.

The three highest per capita consumers of electric power are Canada, Finland and Sweden, all of them cold northern countries with a long dark winter. Canada and the US are in a league of their own in consuming oil, probably because of a heavy reliance on the automobile for commuting and on trucks for moving goods over long distances. In third place, at about 20% lower per capita consumption, are Norway and the Netherlands. This ranking of the Netherlands is a surprise, given the popular image of thousands of Dutch people commuting by bicycle.

The last two rows of Table 1.2 deal with telecommunications, a subject of great importance to Canada because of the very low population density. Canada has more than the median number of telephone land lines per capita but significantly fewer mobile phones. While we obviously have responded to the great need for keeping in touch over long distances, other countries have been quicker to adopt cell phones for remaining connected in densely populated areas.

Excellence in science and engineering

One important determinant of a nation's success in the global knowledge-based economy of the twenty-first century was not included in Table 1.2. Excellence in science and engineering deserves a section of its own.

Science has been a global enterprise for centuries. Scholars around the world openly communicate the results of their basic research, and international peer review is the established instrument of quality control. Senior researchers meet at international conferences and workshops, visit each other's labs, and sit on each other's advisory committees. Postdoctoral fellows move among the world's leading research centres to expand their experience, and it is not rare for graduate students to spend time in research laboratories abroad to learn specific techniques or attend specialist summer schools and like institutions. The best scientific journals are international in the make-up of their editorial boards and the affiliations of the authors who publish in them, and the best textbooks are translated into many languages and used around the world.

In the twentieth century, and particularly after World War II, Canadian engineering research developed in the same pattern, but its internationalization was even faster, enhanced by globalization of industry. Today, the biggest companies are multinational. Supply chains are international, and most high- and medium-technology products contain components made in many countries. In addition, foreign direct investment (FDI) moves both capital and knowledge around the world.

In the last decade, the quality of Canadian science and engineering has taken a leap forward. Sustained new investments, led by the federal government and supported by the provinces, have helped university researchers attain excellence in many important fields. But that excellence is not confined to the universities. It becomes diffused across the economy, largely through students who are taught by active university researchers, and then take jobs in industry and in government laboratories. It is also spread through university-industry research partnerships that involve the companies that are active in R&D and through consulting by individual professors. There will be more to say about this diffusion later, but for now it is sufficient to note that excellence in university science and engineering promotes excellence in science and engineering across the economy. And that has an impact on wealth creation and national prosperity.

A useful indicator of a nation's excellence in science and engineering was proposed by the UK Science Advisor, David King.[8] King counted the number of research papers published by researchers during a specific four-year period, and took its fraction of the total as a measure of each nation's activity in science and engineering. He then applied a demanding quality criterion, counting only those papers that were among the 1% most often cited by other researchers. The fraction of that top 1% contributed by a nation was taken to be the indicator of that nation's excellence in science and engineering. One further step seems reasonable, however. Normalizing the excellence indicator by dividing it by the nation's population makes it a better indicator of the intensity of top-tier activity.

Canada has about $\frac{1}{2}$ of the world's population, produces about 2% of the world's GDP,[9] and publishes more than 4% of the research papers in science and technology. Where does that put us in the group of 23 top economies?

The answer is shown in Figure 1.1, where the ratio of the nation's GDP per capita to the world average is plotted against the indicator of excellence in science and engineering described above. The nations are the same ones as in Table 1.1, except for Mexico and Norway. The prosperity data are for 2005. The four-year period for counting published papers is 1997–2001, which gives a reasonable time lag for the diffusion of new knowledge.

The correlation is very strong because globalization means that there is just one international system of science, engineering, technology, and industry. That system rewards excellence, and it particularly rewards growing excellence on the part of those who started far behind. This is shown in the case of the four BRIC nations—Brazil, Russia, India, and China—that have recently been moving up the value chains of established industries. The actual location of each country on this plot is the result of its economic history; the data are what they are. This is very different from the scatter of measurements in a physical experiment.

One way of interpreting this figure is to say that some countries (such as the US, Japan, Taiwan, and Ireland) are better than average at connecting their excellence in science and engineering with wealth creation. And for whatever reasons, others (such as Israel, Sweden, the UK, and the Netherlands) are not as good as most of the rest of the group.[10] The figure also implies some policy directions. Given its upward slope to the right, a nation must always try to climb the curve by improving the science and engineering excellence indicator, and that means competing on the quality of research. The public sector has the major role in that. However, at the same time, nations must try to improve their capacity for connecting excellent research with wealth creation, and they must strive to move up from the group curve as steeply as possible. That is commercialization, and it is the role of the private sector. Successful innovations in commercialization in one country will be copied by the others,[11] but even so, nobody can afford to stop trying to break ahead of the pack. The public attention paid to innovation and commercialization policies in the 23 economies is a clear sign that governments understand this very well.

Indeed, just this point is made very clearly in the science and technology strategy recently released by the Government of Canada: "Now that we have built a strong research foundation, we must strive for excellence in Canadian science and technology,"

½and "[t]he private sector in Canada needs to do more of what it alone can do, which is to turn knowledge into the products, services, and production technologies that will improve our wealth, wellness, and well-being."[12]

The whole process is like climbing the down escalator. If you slow down, you fall behind.

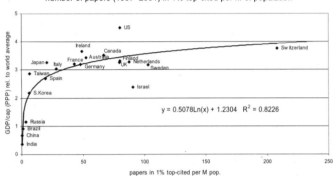

National GDP/cap (PPP–2005) compared to the world average vs. number of papers (1997–2001) in 1% top-cited per M of population

FIGURE 1.1 Prosperity and excellence in science and engineering

But in the competition to establish excellence, there is a cloud on the Canadian horizon. Not enough Canadians earn advanced degrees.

Figure 1.2 shows how Canada and the US have compared in the numbers of degrees granted in all fields from 1993 to 2003 by two university systems that are similar. Comparing degrees granted in all fields removes any ambiguity about the labelling of programs.

The data show that the ratio of Bachelor's degrees followed the ratio of populations closely until the mid-90s, when a gap developed. The situation is more serious at the doctoral level.

There the numbers of Canadian degrees granted lagged behind the US numbers by about 20% over the whole period. One could argue that the US numbers are inflated by the very high proportion of foreign students in US doctoral programs, but that point is moot since many of these foreign students stay in the US and contribute to the nation's competence, which is the real issue in making the comparison.

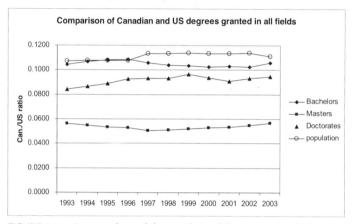

FIGURE 1.2   A comparison of the numbers of degrees granted by Canadian and US universities in all fields

The situation is much clearer at the Master's level. There the Canadian numbers run at about half of the US levels. This situation is particularly serious for two reasons: first, the Master's degree is commonly used for professional upgrading by engineers and other professionals employed in industry. And second, the MBA degree provides the most common route by which scientists and engineers are prepared for management. Canada's lagging performance in this area is a serious situation that must be remedied, as has already been pointed out by others.[13]

The "small country" put-down

All too often we hear the statement, "Canada is a small country. We can't do that." On some measures, Canada is indeed a small country, as the tables above have shown. But in many things that matter, Canada is far from small. Our population exceeds that of many countries (Australia, Finland, Ireland, the Netherlands, Switzerland, Sweden, Taiwan, etc.) that are often held up as examples of success for Canada to learn from. Our huge land holds a rich endowment of natural resources. Our education system is very good and accessible, and we have achieved excellence in many areas of science and engineering. "Canada is a small country," is too easily used—most often by Canadians—as a put-down to squelch the ambitions of other Canadians who are more enterprising and daring. The danger is that Canadians might accept it as conventional wisdom.

Canada's prospects

All things considered, today Canada's prospects are very good. Our economic history brought us prosperity, largely through the sale of commodities: farm products, raw materials extracted from natural resources, and some manufactured products designed elsewhere. More recently, there have been spectacular successes by innovative Canadian companies in the high-tech industries and other sectors as well, but the number of these companies is small—far too small. One thing is clear: in spite of some extraordinary achievements, Canada's current prosperity has not generally been earned by excellence in science and engineering.

On the contrary, our prosperity has made it possible for Canadian science and engineering to achieve excellence. This is a very fortunate state of affairs at a time when commodity producers face increasing competition from third-world countries with much lower labour costs, and when imbedded knowledge is becoming the main source of value-added in more and more products.

Canada has achieved excellence in science and engineering just as this is becoming the key to prosperity. The remaining chapters of this book describe what needs to be done to seize this opportunity to make Canada's prosperity both greater and sustainable.

We must refute once and for all the damning indictment that "Canada is a country that never misses an opportunity to miss an opportunity."[14]

NOTES:

1 There seem to be elements of history and courtesy in Canada's membership in the G-8, but we clearly belong to the "Trillion dollar" club.

2 PPP is the conversion of currencies on the basis of purchasing power rather than nominal exchange rates that may include political influences, or market exchange rates that fluctuate with time. PPP brings prices to a common level, so that one PPP dollar buys the same amount of an appropriately selected "basket" of goods and services in every country.

3 For emphasis, a gap has been left in the table between those countries whose GDP exceeds one trillion dollars and the rest.

4 This idea can be found in the opening words of Adam Smith's great book: "The annual labour of every nation is the fund which originally supplies it with all the necessaries and conveniences of life which it annually consumes, and which consist always either in the immediate produce of that labour,

or in what is purchased from other nations. According, therefore, as this produce, or what is purchased with it, bears a greater or smaller proportion to the numbers of those who are to consume it, the nation will be better or worse supplied with all the necessaries and conveniences for which it has occasion." Adam Smith, "Introduction and Plan of the Work," Chapter 1, page 1, An Inquiry into the Nature and Causes of the Wealth of Nations, New Edition, Adam and Charles Black, Edinburgh (1863).

5   Statistics Canada Reports on the 2006 Census, on their website.

6   The situation in Australia is probably not much different.

7   The data for Table 1.1 were taken from the CIA World Factbook accessed on the Internet in January 2006.

8   David A. King, "The scientific impact of nations," Nature, Vol. 430, 15 July 2004, pp. 311–316.

9   These two numbers suggest that Canada's GDP per capita is about four times the world average. Table 1.1 shows that it's closer to 3.5.

10 These differences can be understood better in the context of the economic history of the respective countries. A recent paper: T. A. Brzustowski, "National prosperity and excellence in science and engineering research," Optimum Online, Vol. 37, Issue 2, June 2007 does this in the form of five pairwise comparisons: Germany vs. Japan, Finland vs. Ireland, the UK vs. Italy, Switzerland vs. Israel, and US vs. Canada.

11 That doesn't necessarily mean that the whole curve will shift upward as a result, since the national prosperity is divided by the world average. So in fact, the curve could shift downward if the less developed economies grew faster

than the developed ones, and the world average (GDP per capita) grew faster than the average for the 23.

12 Government of Canada: "Mobilizing Science and Technology to Canada's Advantage," May 17, 2007, Summary, page 3.

13 "Rebalancing priorities for Canada's prosperity," Report on Canada 2006, p. 31, Institute for Competitiveness & Prosperity, March 2006, ISBN 0-9737377-4-3.

14 Michael Hammer in a speech in Toronto in the late 1980s.

Why Productivity Matters

Productivity is like the weather—everybody talks about it, but nobody does anything. Of course, Canadians know what weather is. (with apologies to Mark Twain)

W hat is productivity and why does it matter? Here is the definition posted on the website of Canada's Department of Finance: "Productivity or Total Factor Productivity: The efficiency with which people and capital are combined in the output of the economy. Productivity gains lead to improvements in the standard of living, because as labour, capital, etc. produce more, they generate greater income."

Discussions of productivity seem to invite vagueness of language. How are people and capital "combined"? And there are other definitions, generally taking productivity to be the measure of some output that one values, per unit of some input that one has to pay for; and this measure can be taken both at the level of the enterprise and of the national economy as a whole. Some people also refer to "productivity" when they're talking about GDP per capita. Still others—mainly in speeches—use the word as a confusing shorthand term for the annual percentage change in productivity. (Perhaps these folks are trying to set an example and become more productive in their own communications by using fewer words.) Everybody tells us that productivity is very important, but few tell us just what it is.

In my view, the productivity of labour is the most intuitive. It is defined as "the value produced per hour of work," and many discussions of productivity in the media and elsewhere deal with that measure of it. Here is a very useful technical note appended to news releases of the US Bureau of Labor Statistics on productivity growth figures:

> **Productivity**: These productivity measures describe the relationship between real output and the labor time involved in its production. They show the changes from period to period in the amount of goods and services produced per hour. Although these measures relate output to hours of work of all persons engaged in a sector, they do not measure the specific contribution of labor, capital, or any other factor of production. Rather, they reflect the joint effects of many influences, including changes in technology; capital investment; level of output; utilization of capacity, energy, and materials; the organization of production; managerial skill; and the characteristics and effort of the work force.

I believe that changing one word in that paragraph, replacing "amount" by "value" in the second sentence, would be a big improvement. It would point the way to raising productivity. But before we go there, let's get an idea of the magnitude of the numbers involved.

The Canadian Centre for the Study of Living Standards tells us that for the year 2004 the Canadian Gross Domestic Product (GDP) measured in 1997 dollars was $1,124,428,000,000—yes, the number of zeros is right. That's over 1.1 trillion dollars! More than 1,100 billion dollars, or more than 1,100 gigabucks!

The Canadian population was 31.9 million, there were 15.9 million jobs,[1] and the people in those jobs worked a total of 27.6 billion hours. That means that in 2004 Canadians worked about 860 hours per year per capita of general population.[2] GDP per hour worked, or the productivity of labour averaged over the entire Canadian economy, was $39.59 per hour.

When we compare that productivity number with the performance of the US on the basis of Purchasing Power Parity (PPP), it turns out that Canadian productivity was only 81.8% of the US value in 2004. And worse, that percentage has been declining. It was 88.4% as recently as 2000. That decline is likely to continue unless we do something, and soon. Our output per hour worked actually declined a bit in 2004, while US productivity grew 3.9% in the same time.

Why it matters

The productivity of labour is the value of what the economy produces per hour worked. That definition immediately shows why, given Canada's demographics, our productivity needs to rise. Since prosperity is measured by GDP per capita, some very simple algebra shows that prosperity equals the productivity of labour multiplied by the number of hours worked per capita.

This is shown clearly by the productivity equation

$$\text{(GDP per capita)} = \text{(GDP per hour worked)} \times \text{(hours worked per capita)}$$

which indicates that prosperity equals the productivity of labour multiplied by the average number of hours worked per capita of general population. The units of time enter into this equation in a subtle way: the GDP per capita and the hours worked per capita both refer to a span of one year.

The hours worked per capita is an average over the whole population, and that means that as the population ages and more workers retire than enter the work force, the number of hours worked per capita of general population will begin to decrease. Early analysis of the 2006 Census has predicted that this would start happening in 2016.

In the meantime, it is instructive to see what has happened in recent years. Table 2.1 shows the number of hours worked per capita and the unemployment rate for the years 2002–2005.

TABLE 2.1   Annual hours worked per capita of the Canadian population

year	2002	2003	2004	2005
annual hrs worked/cap	850	847	862	873
unemployment rate, %	7.7	7.6	7.2	6.8

During the period represented in Table 2.1, the Canadian labour force grew by 760,000 to 17,340,000 and the workforce, or number of people employed, grew by 860,000 to 16,170,000. At the same time, the population grew by almost 900,000 to 32,270,000. The number of employed people grew more than the labour force and almost as much as the increase in population. That explains why the annual hours worked per capita actually increased in 2002–2005. It is hard to imagine that this pattern could be sustained. It would take an extraordinarily good fit of immigration policies and practices on the one hand, and job creation in the economy on the other to head off the decrease in annual hours worked driven by demographics.

Here lies the imperative for raising our productivity. Our productivity must rise just to keep our prosperity constant. It must rise even more to provide the increased prosperity that we need to maintain our high quality of life. And to head off the problem predicted for 2016, we must start now.

How to increase productivity

For the general public, raising productivity can be a scary prospect. It evokes images of lay-offs, of technology replacing people, and of big plants closing in small towns. That, indeed, is the way that many companies must try to remain competitive. This strategy gives them some success on the global scale, but often at a heavy price in their local communities. The companies that typically choose this path are commodity businesses in many sectors: natural resources, agriculture, manufacturing, and services, including even some professional services. Their products are not distinguishable from similar products available from many other sources, and that means that they cannot set their own prices; they must take whatever is offered in the market. And for many commodities, that market price reflects competition from producers in countries with a much lower standard of living than Canada and much lower labour costs.

In many commodity businesses, producers harvest or extract natural resources and export raw materials, and Canadian consumers often find themselves buying products made from these raw materials by workers in other countries who have added value to them. And in that observation lies a clue to the way out of the commodity trap.

The best path is to increase the value added in Canadian products.

There are two business strategies beyond cost reduction that are available to companies in commodity businesses:

increase the volume of production, or increase the value added in the products sold. The former depends on both external and internal factors: the demand for the product and the firm's capacity to increase production volume. The latter is much more of a long-term strategy since it involves developing new skills and engaging new business. But to make things more difficult, two new factors are now complicating the equation, particularly in extraction industries: rising energy costs and greenhouse gas emissions. In general, the extraction of natural resources and the production of commodities from them consumes energy and emits GHG's in proportion to the volume of production. Energy prices have recently been rising steeply, and limits on the emission of GHG's are in the offing. As a result, increasing the volume of production will grow less and less attractive as a business strategy for a large part of the commodity sector of the Canadian economy, even if a short-term boom in some commodity prices suggests the opposite.

For the long term, increasing the value added in products sold is becoming the better business strategy for companies in commodity businesses in all sectors. It also increases the productivity of the whole economy. The best way of increasing productivity is to have more workers engaged in value-added production. This is a long-term strategy that will require new market intelligence, knowledge, skills, and technology. In those companies that succeed, the phrase "learning organization" will be an accurate description of their process of change.

So increasing productivity involves choosing among three strategies:

1. Produce the same stuff with fewer people.
2. Produce more stuff with the same people.
3. Produce stuff of greater value with the same people.

And the best of the three is to produce the stuff of greater value.

Easier said than done? Of course. But it's not impossibly difficult, and in the chapters that follow we shall discuss some practical ways of increasing productivity in this way.

NOTES:

1 13 million full time, and the rest part time. The ratio of jobs to population has been close to $1/2$ for years. It will decline as the population ages.
2 To understand this number, think of half the population working an average of 35 hours a week for 50 weeks.

Getting Started

It's not rocket science.

Row do we start meeting our productivity challenge? In the first two chapters, we saw that Canada must shift from a commodity economy to a knowledge-based, value-added economy. Now we begin to look at how that might be done.

This chapter provides guidance of two kinds. The first is high-level, long-term advice on harnessing a nation's scientific capacity for wealth creation. This advice has been influencing US science and technology policy since the end of World War II, and it is considered by many to have been its recipe for success as an extraordinarily innovative and prosperous economy. Much of this advice is applicable to Canada today.

The second part of the chapter deals with something much more immediate and practical. It demystifies the process of increasing productivity. It's not rocket science. It requires a consistent system of simple, practical measures that everyone can understand. The example chosen to make this point is the Hong Kong Productivity Council, and the list of its activities describes what needs to be done.

The high-level vision: "Science The Endless Frontier"

What has made American industry such an innovative power-house? There are a great many contributing factors, but one document published sixty years ago is widely acknowledged to have been extraordinarily influential.

In late 1944, with the end of World War II in sight, President Franklin D. Roosevelt wrote to his Director of the Office of Scientific Research and Development (OSRD) for advice on how to use science to create a better peacetime. He put the challenge in these words: "The information, the techniques, and the research experience developed by the Office of Scientific Research and Development and by the thousands of scientists in the universities and in private industry, should be used in the days of peace ahead for the improvement of the national health, the creation of new enterprises bringing new jobs, and the betterment of the national standard of living."

The Director to whom the letter was addressed was Vannevar[1] Bush (1890–1974), a distinguished and successful American engineer, inventor, professor, entrepreneur, businessman, and public servant. He had been a professor of electrical engineering and dean at MIT, the co-founder of the Raytheon company in 1922, had developed an analog computer, and proposed some of the concepts of the Internet. As well, he had helped to organize the Manhattan Project, and as Director of OSRD he had coordinated and guided a very large and complex wartime research effort that Roosevelt described as "a unique experiment of team-work and cooperation in coordinating scientific research and in applying existing scientific knowledge to the solution of the technical problems paramount in war."

The response from Vannevar Bush came eight months later. It was addressed to President Harry Truman because Roosevelt had died in the interim. Bush gave it the title "Science The Endless Frontier."[2] The title was very important because it positioned science right in the American tradition of pioneers opening up new frontiers, something the public could immediately grasp. Bush put it this way: "The pioneer spirit is still vigorous within this nation. Science offers a largely unexplored hinterland for the pioneer who has the tools for his task. The rewards of such exploration both for the Nation and for the individual are great. Scientific progress is one essential key to our security as a nation, to our better health, to more jobs, to a higher standard of living, and to our cultural progress."

"Science The Endless Frontier" (STEF, for short) has had an enduring impact. It led to the creation of institutions such as the National Science Foundation (NSF), and of programs that have promoted research excellence and given the US world leadership in research and in technological innovation based on the results of that research. It is the reason why US defence agencies have been supporting an enormous amount of unclassified basic research that has produced major scientific advances in many fields. Its themes have seeped into the nation's scientific, academic, industrial, political, and public consciousness and continue to influence decisions to this day. STEF may be thought of as a statement of the social contract between science and society in the United States.

In Canada we have no such document and no such contract, nor does there seem to be widespread public understanding of the role of science and research in our society. Nevertheless, much has been done by the federal government and the provinces to strengthen Canadian research since 1997, and the quality and scope of Canadian university research in science and engineering are now at an all-time high.

Canada now needs that capacity to meet our productivity challenge. To make our prosperity sustainable in a knowledge-based global economy, we must trade extensively and successfully, facing increasingly demanding customers and increasingly sophisticated competitors. Manufacturing has been very important in Canada and must continue to be very competitive in world markets in terms of both functionality and price, using the most advanced science, the newest technologies, and the best of international business practice to succeed. It is also true that much of our nation's wealth has been derived from natural resources, and we are lucky to have much more in store. But much of the low-hanging fruit in the resource sectors has already been picked, and the ongoing, sustainable exploitation of our natural resources will require sophisticated new engineering and further advances in science. In addition, in the markets for raw materials we also face increasingly capable competitors from countries with much lower labour costs. There are limits to the reductions in production costs that raw material producers can make to stay competitive, as shown by the number of mills and plants that have closed. This means that Canada's quest for competitive advantage has to be shifted from extracting raw materials to producing value-added intermediate goods or finished products. Thus, all the signs indicate that in the future Canada's prosperity will depend much more on our capabilities in science and engineering, and our international business acumen, than it has in the past. To smooth the way for the required efforts in a time of rapid global change, Canada will need appropriate and responsive public policies and government practices.

STEF was written sixty years ago for the US, but there is much in it to guide us today as we acknowledge the need to mobilize our science for a better future. Here are several paragraphs taken from Bush's chapter "Science and the public welfare" that Canadians would do well to take very seriously as we build for the long term.

…We will not get ahead in international trade unless we offer new and more attractive and cheaper products.

Where will these new products come from? How will we find ways to make better products at lower cost? The answer is clear. There must be a stream of new scientific knowledge to turn the wheels of private and public enterprise. There must be plenty of men and women trained in science and technology for upon them depend both the creation of new knowledge and its application to practical purposes.

More and better scientific research is essential to the achievement of our goal of full employment.

THE IMPORTANCE OF BASIC RESEARCH

Basic research is performed without thought of practical ends. It results in general knowledge and an understanding of nature and its laws. This general knowledge provides the means of answering a large number of important practical problems, though it may not give a complete specific answer to any one of them. The function of applied research is to provide such complete answers. The scientist doing basic research may not be at all interested in the practical applications of his work, yet the further progress of industrial development would eventually stagnate if basic scientific research were long neglected.

One of the peculiarities of basic science is the variety of paths which lead to productive advance. Many of the most important discoveries have come as a result of experiments undertaken with very different purposes in mind. Statistically it is certain that important and highly useful discoveries will result from some fraction of the undertakings in basic science; but the results of any one particular investigation cannot be predicted with accuracy.

Basic research leads to new knowledge. It provides scientific capital. It creates the fund from which the practical applications of knowledge must be drawn. New products and new processes do not appear full-grown. They are founded on new principles and new conceptions, which in turn are painstakingly developed by research in the purest realms of science.

Today, it is truer than ever that basic research is the pacemaker of technological progress. In the nineteenth century, Yankee mechanical ingenuity, building largely upon the basic discoveries of European scientists, was able to greatly advance the technical arts. Now the situation is different. A nation which depends upon others for its new basic scientific knowledge will be slow in its industrial progress and weak in its position in world trade, regardless of its mechanical skill.

CENTRES OF BASIC RESEARCH

Publicly and privately supported colleges and universities[3] and endowed research institutes must furnish both new scientific knowledge and trained research workers. These institutions are uniquely qualified by tradition and by their special characteristics to carry on basic research. They are charged with the responsibility of conserving knowledge accumulated in the past, imparting that knowledge to students, and contributing to new knowledge of all kinds. It is chiefly in these institutions that scientists may work in an atmosphere which is relatively free from the adverse pressure of convention, prejudice, or commercial necessity. At their best they provide the scientific worker with a strong sense of solidarity and security, as well as a substantial degree of personal intellectual freedom. All of these factors are of great importance in the development of new knowledge, since much of new knowledge is certain to arouse opposition because of its tendency to challenge current beliefs or practice.

Industry is generally inhibited by preconceived goals, by its own clearly defined standards, and by the constant pressure of commercial necessity. Satisfactory progress in basic science seldom occurs under conditions prevailing in the normal industrial laboratory. There are some notable exceptions, it is true, but even in such cases it is rarely possible to match the universities in respect to the freedom which is so important to scientific discovery.

To serve effectively as the centers of basic research these institutions must be strong and healthy. They must attract our best scientists as teachers and investigators. They must offer research opportunities and sufficient compensation to enable them to compete with industry for the cream of the scientific talent.

And what can be done to strengthen industrial research? Bush's answer is short and sweet:

The simplest and most effective way in which Government can strengthen industrial research is to support basic research and to develop scientific talent. [But] the benefits of basic research do not reach all industries equally or at the same speed. Some small enterprises never receive any of the benefits.

Bush realized that this state of affairs had to be improved with some sort of outreach mechanism. Though he did not develop that idea, the observation was noted and later became the basis of the very successful SBIR[4] program of the NSF.

These statements are as true in the US today as they were in 1946, and they apply to Canada in 2007 as well. They are wise words, and the policies and practices derived from them have worked well in the United States. Canadian governments, universities, and industry should take them very seriously as we develop our own agenda to guide us to increased and sustainable prosperity in the twenty-first century.

The practical approach: Hong Kong Productivity Council

Visions and policies are important, but what do people actually do to raise their productivity? There are many examples around the world of nations taking systematic action to improve their productivity. Hong Kong is a beehive of manufacturing within an intensely competitive business environment. The information provided on the Hong Kong Productivity Council (HKPC) website is very practical, and it takes the mystery out of raising productivity. To begin with, their definition of productivity is very suggestive:

> Productivity is the effective use of innovation and resources to increase the value-added content of products and services. It is the true source of competitive advantage that creates long term economic viability and a better standard of living for all.

The key phrase is "value added." How do we raise our productivity? By increasing the amount of value that Canadians add in what they do. Since productivity is a statistical measure over the whole economy, this will happen even if only a portion of the workforce moves into higher value-added activities. Of course, the bigger the portion the better, and the higher the value added of the new activities the better.

Getting Started

At the level of the enterprise, one can consider increasing productivity by increasing the output per worker with better technology and training, and therefore decreasing the number of jobs required. This is a scary approach, and probably the reason why the word "productivity" does not resonate well with the public. Increasing unemployment is too expensive in many ways and can be very damaging at the local level. At the other extreme, one can try to maintain the number of jobs and increase production, but market conditions, and the increased emission of greenhouse gases (GHG) may make that approach unrealistic. And there are probably strategies in between that combine aspects of the two extremes.

Or one can do something very different—use innovation to increase the value added per worker, and maintain or even increase the number of jobs. At the national level this third strategy must surely be the compelling option. We must strive to increase the value-added content of jobs in every sector of the Canadian economy, and to do that we must have entrepreneurial managers who are constantly on the prowl for opportunities to find ways of adding more value in their businesses.

But if we know how to increase Canadian productivity, why don't we do it? All sorts of business and industry groups, and think-tanks of all persuasions, keep pointing to low productivity growth as a Canadian problem that must be fixed. The Government of Canada announced an Innovation Strategy in 2002; there were lots of discussions across the country, and a national summit at the end of that year… and nothing much since. We seem to be looking for a silver bullet: "if only government lowered taxes and got out of the way," "if only business started investing its profits more in machinery and equipment," "if only our education system were better," etc. But that approach is bound to be fruitless. There is no silver bullet. Instead there must be a patient process of organizing ourselves to enable advances on many fronts and for a long time.

Once again, the Hong Kong Productivity Council provides a useful example of how to proceed. Their website states that

> HKPC's mission is to promote productivity excellence through the provision of integrated support across the value chain of Hong Kong firms, in order to achieve a more effective utilization of resources, to enhance the value-added content of products and services, and to increase international competitiveness.

But the question remains: How do they do this? Here is what they say on their website:

> The Hong Kong Productivity Council (HKPC) is a multi-disciplinary organization established by statute in 1967 to promote increased productivity and the use of more efficient methods throughout Hong Kong's business sectors.
>
> HKPC is governed by a Council comprising a Chairman and 22 members. This Council represents managerial, labour, academic and professional interests, as well as a number of government departments concerned with productivity issues.
>
> HKPC and its subsidiary companies provide a multitude of services to around 3,000 clients each year. The operation of HKPC is supported by fee income from its services and a government subvention in balance.
>
> With 25 Centres of Excellence, 10 testing laboratories, as well as exhibition and training facilities at its headquarters at the HKPC Building in Kowloon Tong, HKPC provides a diverse range of services in manufacturing technologies,

management system, information technologies, and environmental technologies to clients from different industrial and commercial sectors.

As the Hong Kong economy continues to move to higher value-added production, a constant flow of creatively applied technology is essential if the territory is to stay ahead in competitive global markets. To fulfil its role, HKPC is focused on both new technologies and continuous competence development in order to upgrade the performance of its workforce.

Those 25 Centres of Excellence are not research organizations. They are narrowly-focused service organizations where companies find the knowledge they need to meet the detailed needs of their sector. Here are some names indicative of both the focus and the nature of the knowledge provided: Advanced Electronic Processing Technology Centre, Clothing Technology Demonstration Centre, Electromagnetic Compatibility Centre, Intellectual Property Service Centre, Productivity Training Institute, Reliability Testing/Calibration Centre, The Hong Kong Plastic Machinery Performance Testing Centre, etc.

The centres help their clients with what HKPC calls "Eight Pillars of Industry and Support Services." They are as follows:

1. Business Development and Strategic Planning;
2. Technology Transfer and Commercialization;
3. Product Design and Engineering;
4. Business Management Processes and Logistics;
5. Production Technology and Processes;
6. Standards and Quality;

7. Human Resources Management and Development;
8. Other Industry Support Services.

These services are all familiar to Canadian companies, they all make sense, and they're all needed. So working to increase our productivity is not so much about exploring unknown territory as it is about getting our act together and then working to make it a very good act.

It's time for Canadians to stop moaning about our low productivity and do something about it. We need an urgent national effort, and all sectors must play their role in it. Productivity is mainly a private-sector issue, and it's time Canadian industry took the lead in getting the national effort going. The public sector should be a partner, but government shouldn't be expected to pay for the whole thing. Government and education should be ready to join in and help out in playing their appropriate supporting roles, and respond fast enough to make a difference.

It really isn't rocket science!

NOTES:

1 pronounced Van-ee-var.
2 The full text of the report by Vannevar Bush can easily be found on the Internet by searching for "Science The Endless Frontier."
3 It should be noted that American and Canadian terminologies in this area are different. The institutions referred to as colleges and universities by Bush would all be called universities in Canada, as distinct from our community colleges, whose activities are important for the economy but do not include

basic research and education for advanced degrees in the context of research.

4 Small Business Innovation Research program of the US National Science Foundation that helps small businesses participate in US federal R&D and in the commercialization of inventions arising out of federally funded research.

Sustaining our Prosperity

*A prosperous nation has the private and public wealth
to invest and consume in ways that reflect the values of its
people, and thus improve their quality of life.*

The key to sustainable prosperity is sustainable wealth creation in the economy. Wealth creation is the business of business. Wealth is created where value is added, and value is added when a product, whether a good or a service, is sold for more than the cost of the inputs that had to be bought to produce it. The value added provides wages, produces profits, and pays taxes. In this way, it creates both private wealth and public wealth.

In today's global knowledge-based economy, new knowledge originating in science and engineering research is an important and frequent source of added value. That knowledge is imbedded in products and in the processes that produce them, and much of that is done through R&D. This is the case for many goods produced by industry and for knowledge-intensive services. In Canada's case, the domestic market is generally too small to recover today's high costs of research and development of a new product, so success in export sales must be a goal from the outset.

Value added

Two simple equations make the key points about value added. The first one shows how it is created:

value added $=$ sales revenue - cost of purchased inputs

These purchased inputs do not include labour costs for the reason that is made obvious in the second equation, which describes how the value that is added is then used:

value added $=$ wages + profits + taxes

It provides the connection between value added and wealth creation. Wages and profits create private wealth; taxes create public wealth.

The first equation shows that value added does not exist in isolation from a market. It is obvious that value added will be positive only when there is sales revenue that exceeds the cost of purchased inputs. A product may be the best thing since sliced bread, but it creates no wealth unless there are customers willing to buy it at an adequate price.

Time is a very important dimension in business, but the equation does not contain time explicitly. That means that it cannot be used to track value added day by day. The sales revenue from new products usually lags behind the expense of producing them, creating a net cost for an initial period. If a product becomes a money-maker, there is a time when the accumulated sales revenue begins to exceed the total spent on production up to that time. A product is a commercial success if the total revenue significantly exceeds the total production costs over its lifetime.

Such elementary considerations have strategic implications. The definition of value added shows that, on its own, no amount of scientific sophistication and technical competence in creating new products will make Canada wealthy. Our products must be sold to create wealth, and in light of Canada's relatively small domestic market and the high costs of product development, they must be sold profitably on world markets. This means that we must develop our global marketing capacity, explicitly including good global market intelligence, at the same time as we develop our technical capacity for adding value. This must be done in all sectors, including natural resources and manufacturing, to loosen our dependence on commodity exports.

To make this happen, we need the right mix of the right people with the right skills. Excellent researchers must be working at the leading edge of current scientific developments to show the way, and first-rate engineers need to exploit research results from around the world to develop new technologies and ideas for products. Experts in marketing and business must be working to commercialize these products. Canadian businesses in all sectors also have to develop a cadre of entrepreneurial managers who will keep an eye on the long term and always be on the prowl for new opportunities to add value. They must have the long-term market intelligence to position their value-added products where they might best succeed. Canadian business must also develop a pool of well-informed international marketers who will know Canada's potential customers around the world and be able to develop the appropriate business deals; in this connection, our multicultural society should be an ace up our sleeve.

But making our prosperity sustainable requires more. Successes can't be one-off events that persist in memory but fade in the market; they need to keep coming. That requires a full pipeline of new value-added products, positioned for success according to the most up-to-date market intelligence. Existing industries must evolve to maintain success in their markets. New ventures need to be created to exploit entirely new developments. And each generation of Canadian products must be sold at high enough margins to cover the cost of the R&D that produced them, and to invest in the R&D for the next generation.

Which brings us to commodities and innovations.

Commodities and innovations

Commodities are products available from many sources. They have similar properties or functionality, meet the same standards, are of comparable quality, and can generally be substituted one for another. Their prices are set by the commodity markets, and commodity producers have little choice but to take the market price. And therefore, as already discussed, commodity producers rely principally on cost cutting to remain competitive and profitable.

At the opposite end of the product spectrum are innovations. Innovations are new products introduced into the market. They are initially available from one or only very few producers. Innovations are generally quite different from anything already in the market, and some (like the SONY Walkman®) can stimulate a new demand and create a new market. The producers of innovations are able to set their own prices, with margins ideally high enough to pay for the cost of developing them, as well as investing in the R&D for the next new product.

Commodities and innovations can be found in all sectors. Agricultural products, metals, lumber, construction materials, food, household goods, and many manufactured products are commodities. Even the professional services offered by an engineering company that uses routine methods to work on routine projects can be classed as a commodity. But innovations are not just the preserve of the high-tech industry. Innovations in clothing and household goods are marketed routinely, with new designs providing their distinguishing features. And cost-reducing process innovations can be the source of advantage for commodity producers in all sectors.

Furthermore, innovations do not remain innovations forever, or even for long. Successful new products are copied by producers competing in the same market and are gradually turned into commodities. This process is called "commoditization" and is characterized by improving performance, falling prices, and a proliferation of versions of the product under different brand names. For example, the Skidoo® was an innovation as a recreational product in the 1960s, and has long since become a commodity product. The VCR was an innovation 35 years ago, became a commodity in the early 1990s, and is no longer manufactured today. Its successor, the DVD player has become a commodity this decade, as has the personal computer. And the digital camera is becoming a commodity as this is being written.

However, it is also possible for some innovations to last for a long time without becoming commodities, for example, specialty chemicals. These might be products that have a very limited market and are so expensive to manufacture that most competitors stay away from them. Or they may be the products of some proprietary process that has been protected by trade secrets. Once they are too old to be called innovations, they may be called differentiated or specialty products.

When Canada's innovation performance is being measured, generally by surveying the business community, innovations are labelled in three categories: first in the world, first in Canada, or first in the company. Given Canada's dependence on exports, innovations that are first in the world are potentially the most valuable. Innovations that are first in the company may have a global impact as well if the company is a multinational enterprise (MNE), but there is no guarantee that their commercialization will be of particular benefit to the Canadian economy. Innovations that are first in Canada or first in the company are more about keeping up than taking the lead.

For emphasis, in certain parts this book, all products will be labelled as one of the two extremes: commodities or innovations.

A note on the many kinds of innovation

Innovation seems a difficult concept to grasp. I have sat frustrated in many meetings at which busy people spent a lot of time trying to answer the apparently innocent question, "What does innovation mean to you?" The usual outcome was some vague language attempting to accommodate most of the views expressed. I think that the reason for this difficulty is that innovation takes so many forms that the word itself is almost a generic term.[1]

The dictionary definition of innovation has two elements: first, having a new idea and, second, putting it into practice. There is an additional complication because the same word can mean either the action of having a new idea and putting it into practice, or the result of that action.

In the discussion of wealth creation and value added in this chapter, the focus so far has been mainly on product innovations in contrast with commodity products. Innovation was defined as a new product introduced into the market. The corresponding action definition is (the action of) introducing a new product into the market. These definitions are now acknowledged to be those of *product innovation.*

That action definition of product innovation can be restated more crisply as an equation

$$\text{innovation} = \text{invention} + \text{commercialization}$$

where invention is the new idea, and commercialization is putting it into practice.

Process innovation involves materials, methods, and tools (e.g., building aircraft wings by gluing sheets of composite plastic material rather than by riveting aluminum panels). It can be described by the same equation. In that case, the commercialization of the new process involves its competition with existing processes on the basis of cost and performance, for example, quality, throughput, and the potential for enabling the development of new products, etc.

Product innovations come in two flavours: sustaining and disruptive. *Sustaining innovations* improve and sustain an existing product line that meets customers' current needs and makes money for the firm. *Disruptive innovations* are appropriately named. They can undermine a company's existing product but often create an entirely new and much more profitable market. These ideas are very fully discussed by Christensen in his excellent book "The Innovator's Dilemma."[2]

Marketing innovation is another very important category. A good example of this is the appearance of "big box stores" about two decades ago, and a decade before that the introduction of "no-name" and house brands (e.g., President's Choice®) of grocery products when supermarkets moved away from acting as sales agents for manufacturers and towards serving as purchasing agents for consumers.

There are many other kinds of innovation. Here are some whose names provide an obvious description: *organizational innovation, institutional innovation, governance innovation,* etc. Another kind is *complementary innovation,* which consists of the changes in organization, etc. that a firm must make in order to implement successfully some particular product or process innovation.

And most of these innovations come in one of two self-explanatory shades: *incremental innovation* and *radical or revolutionary innovation.*

In all innovation, there is a new idea and it is put into practice. Putting new ideas into practice requires learning new things and abandoning old ones. In the classical words of Schumpeter,[3] this is "creative destruction." In more modern terms, we might speak of people and organizations "reinventing themselves."

The connection between innovation, productivity, and wealth creation

Innovation, productivity, and wealth creation are all connected through value added. Innovations for which producers can set the prices provide the best opportunity to achieve high value added. What generally makes the addition of value possible is new knowledge embedded in the products, whether goods or services. And most of the time, it's R&D that makes the embedding possible.

This might appear most obvious in the case of product innovation in the tech sectors, but I believe that there is room for innovation and increasing the Canadian value added in all sectors. So we need more innovations, more value added, and more R&D in all sectors of industry. And as these activities begin to bear fruit and Canadian producers increase the value added in all sectors, the nation's productivity will rise.

The big picture

Figure 4.1 is a big picture of the flows of knowledge, people, capital, and products between Canada and the world as it exists today. The two arrows at the top show the flows of codified knowledge arising from research. Canadian researchers publish about 4.7% of the world's papers in science and engineering. Being very good at that 4.7% is our ticket to the entire 100%. Research publications from around the world are readily available in libraries and on the Internet, but full access to new knowledge requires knowing that it exists, what it means, how reliable it is, and what can be done with it. And that requires the first-hand knowledge that comes with being active in the world's important research fields.

The two arrows at the 3-o'clock position show the flows of people carrying tacit knowledge in and out of Canada. This is not the place for a debate on whether there is or is not a brain drain today, so these arrows are depicted as equal. The two sets of three arrows each at the 9-o'clock position refer to foreign direct investment (FDI)[4] that simultaneously brings capital, codified knowledge, and new people with their tacit knowledge. For example, when Toyota builds a new plant in Woodstock, Ontario, they invest in the plant and equipment, they bring their technology codified in manuals and software, and they bring in new people with particular management and engineering skills they consider necessary. FDI flowing out of Canada, for example, investments by Celestica or RIM, has the same three dimensions.

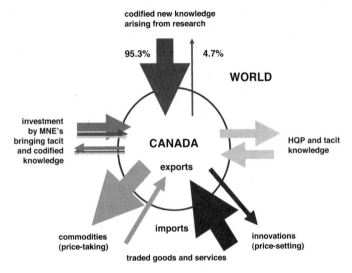

FIGURE 4.1 The big picture

The remaining four arrows at the bottom deal with the way that Canada pays its way in the world: our traded goods and services. At the present time our exports in commodities from natural resources and commodity manufactured products dominate our exports. Their producers must take the world market price. Our exports in innovations, where Canadian producers can set their own prices, are modest compared to our imports of innovations from around the world.

In light of the discussion so far, Figure 4.2 shows a big picture that would be far better for Canada. In that case, the volume of Canadian research is significantly greater than 4.7% (shown as >4.7%). The tacit knowledge brought into Canada by immigrants is shown much increased, primarily through the more effective use of the professional knowledge of immigrants who are already coming here. The growing capacity to add value in Canada has attracted a greater inflow of FDI. The net result is that in the better big picture we have reduced our reliance on exporting commodities and have increased very significantly our exports of innovations. Figure 4.2 shows a Canada whose economy adds much more value than today, a more productive and prosperous country with better prospects for the future.

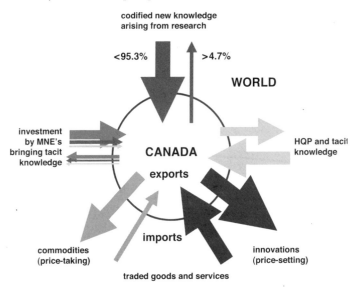

FIGURE 4.2 The better big picture

To make sure that we don't lose sight of our goal in these discussions, the arguments in this chapter can be summarized in one simple diagram. Figure 4.3 shows the desirable sequence of events starting with more and better R&D in Canada, and ending with a better quality of life for people in our country.

better life for people in Canada

↑

more investments and spending that reflect our values: health, children, education, environment...

↑

greater prosperity: more individual and collective wealth

↑

more wealth creation by Canadian business

↑

more Canadian-made innovations and value-added products marketed successfully around the world

↑

more value-added and innovation in all sectors of Canadian industry

↑

more and better R&D in Canada

FIGURE 4.3 Improving life in Canada by improving R&D

NOTES:

1 A historical note: In the Middle Ages, innovation was considered to be a dangerous departure from the established religious doctrine, a step toward heresy punishable by burning at the stake. Innovators are treated far better these days!

2 Clayton M. Christensen, "The Innovator's Dilemma," Harvard Business School Press (1997).

3 The phrase "creative destruction" emerges from the work of Joseph Schumpeter on innovation in the first part of the twentieth century, in which innovation is seen as emerging from a struggle between entrepreneurs and people's resistance to change; see multiple references to it in Jan Fagerberg, David C. Mowery, and Richard R. Nelson: "The Oxford Handbook of Innovation" Oxford University Press, 2005.

4 Portfolio investment is not shown in this diagram.

Time Is of the Essence

"Timing is everything," said the actress to the bishop.[1]

Things are moving faster and faster in the world of business. New products appear, quickly evolve, become commonplace, and disappear, only to be replaced by something newer, better, faster … Trading algorithms enable computers to follow fluctuations in share price and make split-second decisions to buy or sell. New companies appear, grow, dominate their markets, and suddenly reinvent themselves as something quite different. Many companies of all ages disappear. Whole economies emerge into global prominence, as if born full-grown, racing past others that seem to be standing still. But nothing is static, and even those that seem to be standing still are actually working their way up a down escalator. Change is everywhere, continually arriving faster and going deeper.

Nowhere is this more evident than in the consumer electronics industry. As already mentioned in the last chapter, the VCR appeared as an exciting innovation more than three decades ago. There was a brief struggle between the Beta and VHS formats, and VHS won. In the 1990s, the VCR became a commodity product, available as the four-head, hi-fi stereo machine for less than $100 in many brands, including the house brands of store chains. The manufacture of VHS tapes was to stop in 2006, and the only VHS machines to be left on the market were those that could dub VHS tape content onto the next medium, namely the DVD disk. DVD players themselves were introduced only about a decade ago and became a commodity about four years ago. And we already hear the approaching footsteps of another new recording medium of even greater capacity, the next-generation DVD, with another struggle between competing formats. We can keep a record of all these changes with a digital camera, a high-tech product itself now in the process of becoming a commodity.

The Porter Admonition

This pressure for constant change presents a great challenge to business, perhaps nowhere greater than in high-tech consumer goods and services. The following words of Porter and Stern, quoted from the 2002 book *Innovation – Driving Product, Process, and Market Change*,[2] describe that challenge particularly well:

> The defining challenge for competitiveness has shifted, especially in advanced nations and regions. The challenges of a decade ago were to restructure, lower cost, and raise quality. Today, continued operational improvement is a given, and many companies are able to acquire and deploy the best current technology. In advanced nations, producing standard products using standard methods will not sustain competitive advantage. Companies must be able to innovate at the global frontier. *They must create and commercialize a stream of new products and processes that shift the technology frontier, progressing as fast as their rivals catch up.* [emphasis added]

There it is. It's not enough to market a successful innovation; the producer has to keep running to get out the next one, and the next one after that, because competition eventually reduces every innovation to a commodity, and "eventually" is getting sooner and sooner. There's a lot of money to be made in this game because successful innovations can bring high margins, as detailed in the last chapter. But the only way to stay in the game is to keep innovating, refreshing the product to keep it from becoming obsolete, and at some point replacing it with something newer and better. And that can be done only with R&D.

It takes a lot of money spent on R&D to stay in the game. For example, companies that want to thrive in a market that sees new products introduced every year must plan to spend about 16% of sales revenue on their R&D. And the more often new products are introduced, the larger the percentage of sales revenues that must be spent on R&D.

That cuts two ways, of course. A company needs to spend that kind of money on R&D to stay in a fast-moving market. But if it has that much money, or more, for R&D, it has a good chance to become a market leader. Needless to say, both outcomes depend on spending the R&D money to good effect, and that in turn depends on having very good people working on it.

The Innovation Strategy, R.I.P.

In early 2002 the federal government proposed an "Innovation Strategy" with an ambitious and measurable goal. By 2010, Canada was to be fifth in the world on the scale of annual R&D spending per capita. At the time of the announcement, Canada was 15th. The R&D spending was about $20 billion per year, half of that in the private sector and half in the public. The ratio of Gross Expenditure on R&D to GDP, or GERD/GDP, was slipping below 2%, compared with 3 to 4% in the other major economies, and with the goal of 3% averaged over all member countries announced by the European Union.

What would it take to meet the goal of the Innovation Strategy? Obviously, the rest of the world wouldn't be standing still for eight years. Economists who look into crystal balls for a living were able to come up with some rough numbers. They were impressive for some, scary for others. To meet the goal of the Innovation Strategy, Canadian R&D spending would have to be about $50 billion per year in 2010. $20 billion of that would be public, largely from the federal government, and $30 billion per year would be private. In the Innovation Strategy documents, the federal government promised doubling its own contribution, but the private-sector share was left to be found. And that share needed to be massive: a tripling from $10 billion to $30 billion, or an increase of $20 billion per year to be achieved in eight years.

Who would do that $30 billion worth of additional R&D? Additional R&D employees, of course, and lots of them. In 2002, there were about 100,000 R&D employees in Canadian industry. That includes people qualified in the skilled trades, technology, and science at the college diploma and university first degree levels, people with master's degrees, and right up to Ph.D.'s. The average annual spending per R&D employee was about $100,000. Assuming that by 2010 that average spending might increase to $150,000, the number of additional R&D employees required in the private sector by then would be in the range of 100,000. It would take an effective strategy involving universities, community colleges, and immigration to meet this need for highly qualified people in industry. But this is still not the whole challenge. At the same time, the workforce in the public sector, including all the categories of workers listed above and also graduate students and postdoctoral fellows, would have to expand—possibly double—to increase public R&D activity by $10 billion per year.

And where was that new $20 billion for industrial R&D going to come from? Not from the government. With a total annual federal budget of less than $200 billion at that time, of which about a quarter remained for program spending after the national debt was serviced and transfers to governments, institutions, and individuals were looked after, there was no fiscal capacity for that kind of assistance to industry. But even if the fiscal capacity had been there, the political capacity certainly wouldn't have been. And investors don't provide much of the answer either. There are numerous multi-billion-dollar pools of capital, but the additional $20 billion is an annual expenditure— a burn rate, if you will. All things considered, there is only one source of new money for industrial R&D on that scale, and that is an increase in sales revenue on an even larger scale.

How big an increase? To be conservative, assume that the whole sales increase is achieved by the most innovative of Canadian companies, ones that spend 10% of sales revenue on R&D,[3] and come out with new products about every year and a half. Their sales would have to increase by $200 billion per year! That's a huge number, in the range of 15% of current GDP. That kind of growth over eight years is not an unimaginable number, but it would take the co-ordinated effort of industry and government to turn Canada into a world marketing power-house at the same time as we were becoming one of the world's R&D powers.

To help make that happen, government would have to expand its role beyond supporting research and sharing the risk on some industrial R&D. It would have to start helping Canadian companies bring new products to world markets in many more ways. This would need to include tax assistance with product development beyond the experimental development activities that fall under the current program of tax credits for spending on "scientific research and experimental development," the SRED program. It would require assistance with developing market intelligence and with market development that would include strategic procurement to make the federal government the lead customer for new products that meet its own needs. It would demand support of a non-financial sort, involving simpler regulations and faster decisions. And it would also require significant improvements in the transportation infrastructure to speed the movement of Canadian goods to export markets. So if the goal of the Innovation Strategy was to create "Smart Canada, we needed to become "Prompt Canada" as well.

At the same time, for many Canadian companies there would have to be a change in mindset back at the office. Those new sales would have to be largely exports. And to achieve that scale of increase in export sales of new value-added products, there would have to be a new stress on world-first innovations. Company-first innovations might be necessary, and Canada-first would be attractive, but world-first innovations would be essential. The capacity for international marketing of those new products would have to grow at the same time, with a great need for innovation in that domain as well.

Anyway, 2002 has come and gone, and so has the Innovation Strategy, not because it wasn't needed but because … who knows? All the conditions that made it necessary in 2002 still exist in 2007, we've lost five years and some ground, and the requirements for success are still of the same order of magnitude as estimated above. Canadian industry now spends $14 to 15 billion per year on R&D, a number that has remained virtually flat for five years. We continue to see many great Canadian companies doing great things, creating new products and succeeding with them in world markets, but we don't see enough of them. The world continues to change, and Canada can't call time out.

Industrial R&D is changing too. Industry is now finding that it has to spend more and more of their R&D money on the D—developing new products faster. That leaves less and less for the R—research separate from current product development and creating the new knowledge that might be the basis of future product development. There will be more about this in later chapters. But note that this spending trend is changing the time scale of research that industry pays for; the short-term is crowding out the long-term. Industry leaders readily acknowledge the need for basic research as the long-term source of entirely new ideas and of people educated in generating and using new knowledge, but many of them now explicitly state that they can't afford to support it any more, and that basic research must be supported by public funds.

That's not news, of course. Vannevar Bush made that point 60 years ago, and the record of the US economy since then has proven him right.

Forgacs' Conjecture[4]

Several times now, I have linked R&D spending to the frequency of innovation, almost in passing. However, that link is very important to the understanding of industrial innovation, and we will now make it more explicit. It takes a particularly simple and very useful form in Forgacs' Conjecture.

Otto Forgacs had been a senior vice-president of the forest products company, McMillan-Bloedel, in charge of the company's R&D. He has been a thoughtful observer of industrial R&D for many years. Forgacs suggested that companies invest in R&D to keep ahead of their competition in precisely the sense of the Porter Admonition. In other words, they do R&D so that they might always offer innovations in the market, even as their competitors eventually develop products much like theirs and turn the earlier innovations into commodities.

Speed enters the picture through a time scale characteristic of the sector, something Forgacs calls "marketable product life" (MPL). The shorter the MPL, the more quickly new products have to be developed, and the more must be spent on R&D. In that sense, MPL might be thought of as the reciprocal of the frequency of innovation. Normalizing R&D spending by sales revenue to allow for company size gives the R&D Intensity (RDI).

Based on his observations of companies of various sizes in various sectors for many years, Forgacs suggested the correlation shown in the following equation:

$$RDI = 16/MPL$$

where: R&D Intensity (RDI) is R&D spending/sales revenue, given in %

Marketable Product Life (MPL) is in years, and

16 is a parameter obtained by fitting the data

This equation can be thought of as the quantitative form of the Porter Admonition. It shows that companies competing in a market where major new products appear every four years (e.g., new vehicle platforms in the auto industry) must spend 4% of sales revenue on R&D to keep up. In a sector where new products come out every year (e.g., telecom equipment),

16% of sales are spent on R&D. Conversely, in a sector where companies spend less than 1% of revenue on R&D, products last a couple of decades with little change (e.g., natural resource industries). In simple terms, companies with a higher R&D intensity innovate more frequently than those with a lower intensity.

Clearly, the concept of an average marketable product life doesn't fit equally well in all cases. For example, in the early years of a research-based start-up company there are few products and limited revenues, but there may be a great deal of R&D if the whole field is moving fast. Here, MPL could be thought of as the time between major milestones, a few months more likely than years, and the logic of Equation 5.1 still seems relevant. For such companies, RDI may significantly exceed 100%, and they must be financed to continue to do research and product development. As shown below, this happens frequently, and it points the way to understanding another aspect of the time dimension in innovation.

The cadence of innovation in industry

Forgacs' Conjecture suggests that the R&D Intensity (RDI) might be very useful in studying the dynamics of innovation in industry. The RDI is readily calculated from reported data on R&D spending and sales revenue; it is the ratio of the two. Any two of those numbers yield the third. However, the RDI introduces additional information through its connection to the frequency of innovation as described above.

Figure 5.1 is a plot of longitudinal data about the pharmaceutical and biotech companies that are among Canada's Top 100 R&D Spenders. The data are the annual values of RDI plotted on a log scale. They were taken from the very useful annual publication by RE$EARCH Infosource.[5] The data cover the years 2000 to 2005, inclusive. Forty-seven companies in this sector appeared among the Top 100 at some time in that period, and every such appearance is marked by one of the annual symbols. Each one of the companies shown spent at least $14 million[6] on R&D each year.

The first thing to note is that the companies fall into two groups. Almost precisely one half of them always had the RDI well below 100%. The other half exceeded 100% in at least one year. The companies with RDI below 100% showed little variation from year to year. Indeed, companies 5 to 19 appear to be clustered around an RDI of 10%. They can be called the "mainstream" of the sector, and here the mainstream MPL is about 1.6 years, or 19 months. So the mainstream of the Canadian pharma/biotech sector produce new products on the average about once every year and a half or so.

To the left of the mainstream are several companies that innovate less frequently, with the lowest one introducing a new product every four years or so. These companies might be called the "commodity end" of the sector.

The mainstream and the commodity end show little variation in RDI over the six years, and they can be described as operating in the steady state. This does not suggest an absence of growth, just the fact that the companies operate in a pattern that changes little with time.

The right half of Figure 5.1 is very different. The companies shown there often spend more on R&D than their sales revenues, sometimes many times more.[7] Moreover, their RDI varies very significantly from year to year. This is a very volatile region. Some companies drop out of it; new ones enter it. These companies are being financed to do R&D to develop new products. They deal with rapid change: some in their knowledge base as new research results come out, some in their target market, and some of their own making. Their behaviour can be labelled "transient."

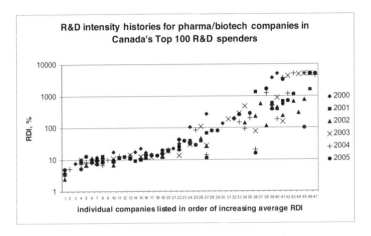

FIGURE 5.1 Innovative companies in pharma/biotech showing steady-state and transient behaviour

The pharma/biotech sector is the largest group in the Top 100, but similar behaviour can be seen among the companies from other sectors.[8] The big difference is that the values of RDI are much lower in many other sectors, such as natural resources, materials, and energy.

The steady-state and transient companies have what I will call a different cadence in their business. And differences in cadence at the company call for differences in cadence on the part of those who deal with them. Consider, for example, a program of government support for R&D. The steady-state companies might be well served by a steady program in which many applications to an agency were all filed by a certain date, evaluation and decision followed at a measured pace, and money eventually flowed to successful applicants.

But that would not work for the transient group. They ride up and down the waves of change. They need quick decisions by people who see and understand their constantly changing situation. They would be served best by "account executives" assigned to them, riding the waves with them, and authorized to make timely decisions. For companies in the volatile region, particularly the smaller ones, such timely response could be a matter of survival.

There is one more thing to notice in Figure 5.1—a tip for investors among the readers. Consider company #27. Its RDI fell continuously from about 300% to the mainstream value of just over 10% in the six years. The full data show that this did not happen because of reduced R&D spending. It happened because sales revenues grew much faster than R&D spending. Clearly, this is a company that is succeeding with the products it developed. The same behaviour of RDI is the hallmark of successful new ventures in the other sectors.

Wasted time

To conclude the discussion of the time dimension in innovation, it is useful to consider unproductive or wasted time. As has just been noted, such wasted time can create very serious problems for the transient companies that must survive in an environment of rapid, and often sudden, change. For that matter, it undoubtedly also presents obstacles to those operating in the steady state.

Here are some sources of unproductive time in the environment where business must operate:

- Traffic jams delaying the road transportation of goods;
- Physical and bureaucratic bottlenecks in sea, air, and rail transport;

- Job action caused by delays in negotiating new labour contracts after the expiration of previous ones;
- Delays in the approval processes of government funding agencies;
- Delays in the legal system;
- Delays in the commercial financial system;
- Delays in routine processing and approval transactions at all levels of government caused by inadequate staffing or training, or both;
- Decision delays by tribunals and other regulatory bodies because of inadequate capacity or incomplete membership;
- Slow transfer of routine information within and between agencies of all kinds.

There is an economic price to pay for all of these sources of delay. Given the importance of time in business, they have no place in "Prompt Canada."

I leave it to the reader to complete the list with some personal pet peeves.

NOTES:

1 ...or was it the bishop to the actress?

2 Michael E. Porter and Scott Stern, in Edward B. Roberts (ed.), *Innovation – Driving Product, Process, and Market Change*, p. 239, Jossey-Bass, 2002.

3 This really is very conservative. The 100 companies that spend the most on R&D in Canada, average slightly less than 5% of sales revenue spent on R&D.

4 In an environment well sprinkled with economists, I had been calling this relationship Forgacs' Law. But having followed some recent developments in mathematics, I have taken to calling it Forgacs' Conjecture. It was most recently discussed in the paper by Otto Forgacs, "Who spends money on R&D

and why?" presented at the Forum "R&D—The Ticket to Wealth Creation," Conférence de Montréal, June 7, 2004. The author first heard the main idea when Dr. Forgacs spoke about it in the author's presence at a meeting of the National Research Council of Canada in 1997.

5 "Canada's Corporate Innovation Leaders," is a well-known report published annually by RE$EARCH Infosource Inc. and distributed as a supplement to numerous daily newspapers in early November in the last three years, and in early July in earlier years. The data consist of the reported values of current and previous year R&D expenditures and current revenues, and the calculated values of percentage change in R&D spending and the R&D Intensity (RDI), i.e., here the ratio of R&D spending to revenue expressed as a percentage. The companies are listed in order of decreasing R&D expenditure. The data for each year contain only a few gaps (typically about 10) where revenue was not reported and RDI could not be calculated. The companies are grouped by industry in these 16 categories (listed alphabetically): aerospace, automotive, chemicals and materials, communications/telecom equipment, computer equipment, electrical power and utilities, electronic parts and components, energy/oil and gas, forest and paper products, health services, machinery, mining and metals, pharmaceuticals/biotechnology, software and computer services, telecommunications services, and transportation.

6 The lower cut-off for membership in the Top 100 R&D spenders stayed very close to $14 million per year over the whole six years.

7 The very high values of RDI at the right edge of Figure 5.1 were arbitrarily capped at 5,000%.

8 T. A. Brzustowski, "R&D intensity as a basis for R&D support policies," Optimum Online, Vol. 37, Issue 1, April 2007.

CHAPTER 6

Innovation in Canadian Industry

"Wealth is generated most abundantly by producing tradable articles in which knowledge is embodied." —*John A. Schey*

The box shown below appeared in The Wall Street Journal on July 11, 2007.[1]

Philips Rx

- **The situation:** As their core products become commodities, technology pioneers like Philips have looked to new areas, such as health care, for growth.

- **The background:** Philips's medical systems unit has long made big equipment for hospitals. A new consumer-health division aims to directly target consumers - especially the elderly.

- **What's at stake:** Mainly a seller of products, Philips must now learn to market services in order to win on the health-care front.

The company in question is Royal Philips Electronics NV, a Dutch MNE (multinational enterprise) that had been one of Europe's greatest successes, first in the electrical and then in the electronic industries. Philips has a great record of producing innovations, including the ubiquitous audio cassette introduced in 1963.

The box has some important things to say about industrial innovation. First, it points out that even a great technology company has to face the fact that its innovations eventually become commodities, as has already been discussed in Chapter 5. Second, it describes Philips adopting a new business model for future success, redirecting the company to a new market based on one of their established product lines. Third, it shows that to serve that market, they will move into offering services,[2] blurring the traditional distinction between manufacturing and services. And finally, it shows the growing market influence of demographics and the aging of the population.

The box reproduced above offers a good introduction to a discussion of innovation in industry.

There are some excellent books providing managers with insight and guidance on industrial innovation,[3] and it is not our intention here to venture into that space. Rather, we will consider some aspects of innovation and R&D, the role of design in D, the R&D spending by Canadian industry, and finally the road ahead.

The impacts of different sectors

To begin, let us consider the impact of the various sectors of industry on the Canadian economy.

TABLE 6.1 Relative economic impact of the main sectors of industry [4]

Industry sector	Share of GDP, %	Composition of businesses	% of GDP share exported	% of GDP exported	% of total employment
Manufacturing	16	transportation eqpt. 16%, food 10%, chemical 10%, fabricated metal 8%	50	8	13
Oil and gas and mining	4	energy 62%, mining 25%	88	3.5	1.5
Services to households	12	retail trade 52%, others services exc. public admin 21%, food services 19%	7	0.8	25
Services to business (information, cultural, professional, scientific and technical—ICPST)	9	PST services 52%, IC 48%	12	1.1	9
Other services to business	14	wholesale trade 47%, transportation and warehousing 35%, admin. support, waste management and remediation 17%	18	2.5	13
Construction	6	engineering, repair and other 49%, residential 33%	0	0	6
Other primary industries	2.3	crop and animal production 63%, forestry and logging 27%	56	1.3	2.6
Utilities	2.5	electric power generation, transmission, and distribution 82%, natural gas distribution 11%	5	0.12	0.7

Table 6.1 shows that manufacturing is the leading exporting sector by far, with oil and gas, and mining placing a distant second. It is very interesting, however, to note that ICPST and other services to business together export as much value as the oil and gas, and mining industries. However, things look different in our balance of international payments.[5] In 2006, for example, Canada's balance of payments in goods and services was $36.1 billion, made up of a positive balance of $51.3 billion in goods and a negative balance of -$15.1 billion in services, mainly in travel and transportation.

One more statistic will be useful. Industry Canada (see note 4) also reports the change in the contributions of various industries in the manufacturing sector to real GDP since the end of 2001. These are shown in Table 6.2. Nine industries decreased their contributions. What they have in common is that they all make commodity products.

Eleven other industries increased their contributions to GDP over the same period. Many of these industries, particularly the ones with the highest increases, produce innovations and differentiated products. We shall come back to these observations later in discussing a long-term strategy.

Griller's Framework

Thirteen years ago, David Griller[6] proposed a framework for industrial innovation in Canada that is useful for guiding our thinking. It classifies industrial innovators into four categories, and applies equally to product and process innovations. The categories are: science-based, high-tech craft firm, systems integrator, and flexible technology purchaser.

There are three further classifications of innovations that are very useful: (1) the distinction between manufacturing and services, (2) between traded and untraded[7] products, and (3) among innovations that are world-first, Canada-first, or company-first.

TABLE 6.2   Changes in the contribution to real GDP since 2001 for various industries in the manufacturing sector

Industry	Change in the industry's contribution to real GDP, %	Industry	Change in the industry's contribution to real GDP, %
Computer and electronics	+40	Leather and allied products	-52
Miscellaneous	+22	Textile mills	-42
Chemical	+17	Clothing	-27
Wood	+17	Electrical equipment	-23
Transportation equipment	+7.5	Textile product mills	-13
Machinery	+7	Beverage and tobacco	-12
Non-metallic minerals	+7	Printing	-11
Fabricated metal	+5	Furniture	-9
Petroleum and coal	+4	Paper	-6
Primary metal	+2		
Food	+<1		

Services, in turn, can be divided into services to households and services to business. Combining these distinctions with Griller's four categories gives us a framework of different kinds of innovation that, in theory, can number 72.[8] Fortunately, far fewer need be considered, since not all combinations make sense. For example, the makers of products only for the domestic market are not likely to invest in developing world-first innovations. And producers of services to households seem much more likely to innovate by purchasing technology than in any of the other three ways.

While the four categories in Griller's framework are listed as separate, they are not mutually exclusive, in the sense that more than one of them might be found in any innovative enterprise. Since innovation is invention with commercialization, the four kinds of innovation might be expected to differ both in the source of invention and in the process of commercialization.

1. Science-based: The inventions of research-based innovators arise from their own research results, or from those of others obtained by reading the open scientific literature. Some established companies in high technology and many in pharmaceuticals/biotechnology, as well as start-ups in both areas, depend on research-based innovation for their competitive advantage; but commercialization is much easier for the established firms with established market reach. The innovations are likely to be in traded goods and services with export potential, since the cost of developing entirely new products starting from research results can be very high, and the Canadian market is too small for recovering them. Patents, licenses, and IP (intellectual property) management are important for research-based innovators. In the case of established companies with substantial R&D capabilities, the original invention can trigger a cascade of related enabling inventions that are patented and become the basis of a whole range of new products. This is very difficult to achieve in the case of a start-up based on a single invention.

2. High-tech craft firms: In a craft firm the source of competitive advantage lies in the skills and knowledge of its workers. Inventions can arise in the course of making things, and trade secrets are generally more important in protecting the IP than are patents. Expensive projects with markets for only a limited number of units, (e.g., satellites in the aerospace sector,) provide one example. Such innovations are generally traded goods. They may be final products, or components for someone else's system, or even process innovations in the form of new tools. At the other end of the spectrum of technological complexity is innovation by design or redesign. There the high-tech aspect of the craft probably resides more in the tools than in the products. The design department of a manufacturing company may be its main source of competitive advantage. Other examples of craft shops that depend on design to produce innovations in goods or services include advertising agencies, designer clothing studios, custom boat builders, etc. Depending on the ingenuity of the workers and on the particular markets served, world-first, Canada-first, and company-first innovations by craft firms are all possible, but some are much more likely than others.

3. Systems integrators: Their inventions are made possible by the availability of products—artifacts, software, tools, etc.— available from suppliers. The system integrator contributes skills in analysis, design, adaptation, assembly, etc., as well as proprietary tools and methods that might come out of their own R&D. Innovation can take the form of developing a custom solution that uses available software and hardware components to meet one client's particular needs and is sold as a one-off system (e.g., a custom IT system for a company). In that case, the innovation might be seen as a service provided by the vendor. At the opposite end of the volume spectrum, the innovation of a system integrator might be the design of a final product and its manufacture by integrating components from many suppliers, including some in-house (e.g., auto final assembly). In that case, the system integration would be counted as manufacturing. Lead time over the competition is the way such innovations are protected. World-first, Canada-first, and company-first innovations by system integrators are all possible.

4. Flexible technology purchasers: In this case, inventions arise from new uses of technology already available in the market. The biggest companies offering new service products created in this way are in telecommunications. In the case of SMEs,[9] process innovations developed using the purchased technology seem more likely than product innovations. In either case, world-first innovations of either kind are unlikely, but not impossible. It all depends on the depth and ingenuity of the technology purchaser's technical people, and their capacity to increase the added value in their products by the use of technology that is available to others as well. Canada-first innovations are more likely, particularly when the purchasers are among the first in the country to acquire the new capability, and marketing can often be the main means of maintaining advantage. Examples might be a new food-packaging technology that is a process innovation in the grocery business, or a new sawmill technology for the lumber industry. Technology purchasers can innovate in manufacturing or in services, in traded or domestic sectors; process innovations in commodity businesses to reduce costs are common. However, if they have substantial R&D capacity of their own, they can use purchased technology to create significant product innovations in any sector. And if they work closely with the producers of the technologies they purchase, world-first innovations may not be out of reach, (e.g., companies buying production equipment for "fabs" in which they manufacture microelectronic computer chips).

The R and the D of R&D

Contrary to the impression that might be given by frequent joint labelling in economic statistics, "R&D" is not one thing. Research and development are two closely related but very different activities carried out by different people working in different places, within different cultures, for different purposes, at very different costs, and with very different risks. The expenditures reported under "R&D" spending are made up of two components that are not interchangeable, and are balanced very differently in the public and private sectors.

At the highest level, research may be defined as the process of learning that which is unknown to anyone, anywhere. As used in R&D, development is defined[10] as "the process of working up (an idea, product, etc.) for marketing etc." It is an essential step in the commercialization of new products. The contrast between research and development is evident from the definitions, but it is more useful to show the differences in a list of the main features of the two processes. This is shown in Table 6.1. Evidently, it makes little sense to talk about R&D at universities. There is only research at universities, and no products are developed there. Contrived expressions such as "Big R and little d" or "little r and big D," take only a small step toward greater precision.

In reality, the cultures of research and development are so different that connecting them is difficult even within one corporation driven by a single set of goals. It is even more difficult when the task is to transfer the results of research from a university, whose goal is to create and transmit knowledge, to a corporation whose goal is to create wealth. Nevertheless, in Canada we have been learning how to do this, and we're starting to get good at it.

Recent changes in industry have produced some paradoxical changes in the relationship between R and D. At one time, many major corporations had their own basic research labs. These were the sources of new knowledge and ideas for the companies' long-term growth. Among the best known were the Bell Labs in Murray Hill, N.J. and the General Electric Research Laboratory in Schenectady, N.Y., in both of which Nobel Prize winners could be seen in the corridors.

However, most companies can no longer afford to support basic research. Because of the faster and faster commoditization of their products in the market, and the need to produce innovations more and more quickly in response, most companies have had to bring the capabilities of their researchers to bear on product development. Their R has come much closer to their D, and the earlier concern with ideas for tomorrow has been sacrificed to meeting the market pressures of today. This has produced organizational and cultural changes in which research capacity has been changed and inserted into product development, and embedding new knowledge in new products has been accelerated. In the terminology used here, project research has replaced basic research.

Paradoxically, the changes that have brought research and development closer together in industry have created a greater separation between industry R&D and university research. The universities, and some government laboratories, have now assumed the responsibility for basic research—at public cost, of course. This poses a particular challenge to Canadian universities. They must combine this new level of responsibility for basic research with the need to undertake project research in areas where Canadian industry needs help, as will be shown in the next chapter.

TABLE 6.3   Research and development are very different

Research
- long-term programs of exploration and discovery
- in Canada done mostly in the public sector, with some exceptions
- mainly the work of scientists, and some engineers
- involves theory, experiment, and verification
- consumes wealth
- risk is scientific, and kept to a minimum through scientific peer review
- open publication of results, international flows of information, some patents
- successful research always leads to more research; it may also produce important and revolutionary innovations, but they are rare and unpredictable

Development
- short-term projects with specific goals, often driven by market feedback
- private sector activity essential to commercialization and innovation
- mainly the work of engineers and some scientists
- involves design and building of prototypes, testing and improvement, design for production
- consumes wealth, generally much more expensive than research
- risk is financial, and kept to a minimum through due diligence and good business practice
- information closely held and protected: trade secrets, many patents
- successful development projects lead to innovations and new wealth creation through sales of new goods or services

The role of design

The discussion of the four categories of innovation suggests an additional way of looking at them. Craft shops, system integrators, and technology purchasers all engage in market-driven innovation. They respond to signals from the market. Research-based innovators are driven by new knowledge.

Figure 6.1 shows the differences. Research results play a big role in research-based innovation and only a small role, if any, in market driven-innovation. And in the latter case, this might likely be market research rather than scientific research. On the other hand, market feedback is a big factor in market-driven innovation. Market forecast is important in both research-based innovation and market-driven innovation, but the feedback is available only in the latter case.

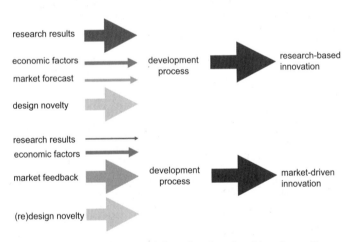

FIGURE 6.1 Comparing research-based and market-driven innovation

Design is a key element of both kinds of innovation. It may be the design of an entirely new product, or the redesign of an existing one. Design is the intellectual creative activity of engineers, but not only of engineers. In this context, it should be thought of as the solution of a particular problem under a set of constraints, and embodying that solution in an appropriate artifact, system, or service. The designer's first task is to study the needs of those whom the design is to serve, the environment in which it is to function, and the constraints under which that must be done. Cost is always a constraint, but only one of very many different ones. The needs to be served suggest the functionality of the design. The environment has many dimensions: physical, ergonomic, legal, cultural, etc.

The designer's challenge is different in the two cases. In research-driven innovation, the designer must develop an entirely new concept that will embed the new knowledge and transform it into the desired functionality to serve the customer. In the market-driven case, the designer must start with the existing product and improve the design in a way that will respond to the market feedback. The economic factors are different in the two cases. The challenge with research-based innovation is the large and risky up-front investment required to launch a new product to an unknown reception. The economic factors are less challenging when the market for the product is well known and the product is responding to demand, even if it is new. A redesigned, improved product carries even less risk. It has already been on the market, the marketing channels are established, and its sales record is known.

Figure 6.2 shows the factors influencing design in market-driven innovation. The word (re)design is used to show that these ideas apply both to the design of new products or the redesign of existing products to improve them.

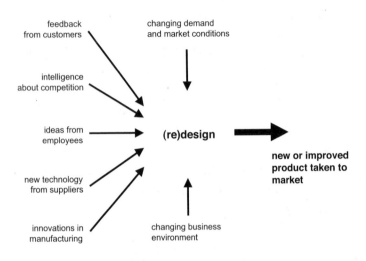

FIGURE 6.2 Design in market-driven innovation

At this point it may be useful to review the Glossary (p. 171), which gives the precise meaning of some important words used in this chapter. Imprecise use of common words such as technology[11] and innovation can sometimes lead to confusion and misunderstandings.

The cost of R&D

Compared with the other advanced industrialized economies, Canadian industry spends relatively little on R&D. This is indicated by BERD/GDP, i.e., the business expenditure on R&D measured as a fraction of the country's GDP. For Canada in 2004, BERD/GDP was about 1.15%.[12] This compared with a high of almost 3% for Sweden, 2.4% for Finland, and 1.85% for the US. Of the countries included in the comparisons in Chapter 1, only the UK and the Netherlands were lower than Canada, but still above 1%. China came in at 0.85%, but with its BERD growing at over 20% per year, it will quickly move up in the ranking.

The dollar amount of Canadian business spending on R&D in 2004 was $14.4 billion. This sum supported the work of 126,700 employees, providing wages and salaries, current operating costs, and capital expenditures. This works out to an average annual expenditure of $114,000 per employee.

The R&D spending by Canadian industry is highly concentrated. The top one hundred R&D spenders are responsible for about 75% of the total. Even so, only the top company in that group, Nortel Networks, has ever made it into the world's top 100. And within the Canadian Top 100, the Top 10 companies account for two-thirds of industrial R&D spending, or half of the national total. The cut-off for the Top 100 has been at an annual R&D spending between $14 and 15 million for several years. That means an R&D establishment of 100 to 150 people.

These numbers, of course, say something about the rest of the economy. There are 600 large establishments in the goods-producing sectors of the Canadian economy and 109 in professional, scientific, and technical services,[13] 609 of them obviously outside the Top 100 R&D spenders. If all the remaining business R&D in Canada were concentrated in these 609 establishments, it would involve at most 31,600 R&D employees engaged in an effort worth about $3.5 billion. On the average, then these large establishments might operate with 52 R&D employees engaged in a $5.7 million enterprise. Since some medium enterprises and even some small ones are also engaged in R&D, these averages are actually smaller. This all adds up to a strong impression that in the large majority of Canadian companies the R&D capacity is spread very thin, much thinner than the weak national BERD/GDP would suggest.

As pointed out in Chapter 4, a useful indicator of business R&D spending is the percentage of revenues spent on R&D, the so-called R&D Intensity (RDI). It introduces the connection between R&D spending and the frequency of innovation. In general, average RDI varies greatly from sector to sector. For example in 2003, it ranged from a high of 14% in the pharmaceuticals, biotechnology, medical devices and instruments sectors, to a low of 0.67% in natural resources and commodities. According to the Forgacs formula described in Chapter 5, this would mean a range of innovation frequencies from about one a year at the top to about one every two or three decades at the bottom.

Comparing this performance with the top R&D spending companies in the US and in the world reveals that Canadian companies as a group innovate the least frequently, and their sales revenues depend the least on new products.[14]

Now what?

Various explanations have been offered for this state of affairs. "It's all in the structure of our industry," some will say. "We are strong in areas that don't require much R&D." Others point to the large number of branch plants in Canada, in industries whose R&D is done in the US and elsewhere. Interprovincial trade barriers, and federal-provincial relations that are not always as constructive as they need to be, have been identified as part of the problem. Social commentators decry Canadians' lack of entrepreneurship and aversion to risk. Management education for too few, and maybe of the wrong sort, and a weak culture of commerce have also been identified as contributing factors. And there is always something that government has done, or failed to do, that can be assigned blame for the latest shortcoming.

There's some truth in all of that, but explaining the situation in so many ways too easily turns into justifying it.

The fact remains that we are in the state that we're in, and we need to change.

The strategy of Philips cited at the beginning of this chapter has lessons for Canadian industry as well. The manufacturers of commodity products have not been doing well, as shown in Table 6.2. Philips reacted to the commoditization of their products by seizing a business opportunity provided by the conjunction of two factors: their experience in high-tech hospital equipment, and the aging of the population. Their solution was to create a new line of business based on a new product aimed at the needs of the elderly living at home—a smart personal monitor and alarm—and providing the communication services that connect it with the health care system.

This business model is not new. For example, RIM does the same thing in selling the BlackBerry® handset through telcos and then working with them to deliver the BlackBerry® service to consumers. The BlackBerry® is a manufactured product with "a long service tail," and the Philips monitor has the potential to become one as well.

The Canadian manufacturers of commodity products should follow the lead of Philips, and begin reducing their dependence on commodities by innovating and introducing value-added products. This will not be easy. Their new business opportunities are not likely to be as clear-cut as in the case of Philips, and their R&D capabilities will most likely be far inferior, so they may need help. A few of them might be able to take advantage of the growing need for services in an aging population, but most may be limited to moving up the value chain of their present businesses. If they succeed, they will do themselves a lot of good, and contribute to raising Canada's productivity in the process. The alternative is to stay in the commodity business and keep trying to cut costs.

Value-added manufacturing in the big picture

How good is that last advice? Is it telling people to board a sinking ship? With the growth of services in the Canadian economy, the outsourcing of production to Asia, and the rise of the Canadian dollar relative to the US dollar, is Canadian manufacturing of any kind—commodity or value-added—not in imminent danger of becoming uncompetitive and unimportant, and disappearing from view?

The answer to all these questions is that value-added manufacturing is so important to the economy, both directly and indirectly, that we must make every effort to help it continue in a healthy and vigorous form. That does not mean that it should continue without change, but it does mean that its huge contribution to the economy must be understood, maintained, and even increased.

These are strong statements, and in their support I cite the very authoritative book[15] by John Schey, one of the world's great manufacturing engineers. Written at the University of Waterloo in Canada, this book has been translated into the languages of many of the industrialized nations of the world and has become one of the world's most influential engineering textbooks. In its three editions, it has been used by hundreds of thousands of mechanical engineering students on their way to becoming production engineers. The following paragraph taken from Schey's introductory chapter tells the story with striking clarity:

If one analyzes the components of the GNP, it is evident that the material wealth comes from only two substantial, basic sources: material resources and the knowledge and energy that people apply in using these resources. Agriculture and mining are of prime importance, yet they represent only 3-8% of the GNP of industrially developed nations. Manufacturing claimed the largest single share until the 1950s. Since then, much of the growth has taken place in the service sector, and recent data…would suggest that - at least in highly developed economies - material wealth is independent of the contribution of manufacturing to the GNP. This, however, is an illusion. What the numbers fail to show is that increasing wealth is based on an increasingly sophisticated manufacturing sector; this in turn creates the need for many similarly sophisticated supporting activities such as research, design, and financial services, distribution, mainte-nance, and field service of products, and even the hospitality and travel industry connected with manufacturing. For statisti-cal purposes, all these supporting activities are classified as services. Yet, unless a nation is exceptionally well endowed with natural resources, a strong service sector can exist only if there is a similarly strong manufacturing sector. Only the interactions of the two can secure competitive advantages in a global economy where the simpler tasks migrate to low-wage environments. It is often said that, in the information age, knowledge is the most valuable commodity. This is quite true, but it is also true that knowledge itself can be bought relatively cheaply. Wealth is generated most abundantly by *producing tradable articles in which knowledge is embodied.* [emphasis in the original]

That last sentence expresses the main idea on which this book is based.

A distinctive feature on Canada's R&D landscape

To complete this look at industrial R&D in Canada, we need to note two relatively recent institutional innovations that are already proving to be very valuable. They both rely on the ability of Canadians to create effective national networks of university researchers and their partners in industry and government. One such innovation is the program of Networks of Centres of Excellence (NCE), and the other is the "4th Pillar" organization, the first three pillars being industry, government, and academe.

The 4th Pillar organizations are independent, not-for-profit corporations that leverage private and public funding to assemble networks of strong university-industry R&D collaborations and partnerships on a national scale. They focus on developing complementary industrial and university capacity in specific sectors, in order to achieve both world-class excellence in research and competitiveness in high-tech industry. They do this by sponsoring project research that exerts a market pull and involve students in working at the state-of-the-art, and by providing the most modern tools for them to use in their research and their studies. There are three 4th pillar organizations, and it is a measure of their success that each one has been instrumental in helping Canadian industry to achieve prominence in an important area of high technology: CANARIE Inc. in broad-band communications networks, CMC Microsystems in microelectronics and the broader area of microsystems, and Precarn Inc. in artificial intelligence and robotics.

The NCE program is larger in scale and broader in scope. For example, in 2004–2005, there were 21 individual networks. The typical one involved between 50 and 100 professors from several dozen universities in Canada and abroad, as principal investigators supervising the research of 200 to 300 graduate students, postdoctoral fellows, research associates, and technicians. The small administrative centre of each network is tucked away on one host campus. Each network deals with one problem area, generally approaching it in a broad and multidisciplinary way, with partners from industry and government. The problem areas include environment, health, and technology. For example, the first five in the alphabetical list are networks on Advanced Foods and Materials; on Allergy, Genes, and Environment; on Aquaculture; on the Arctic; and on the Automobile in the 21st Century. The Canadian Stroke Network deals with topics ranging from the basic science of the causes of stroke to protocols for urgent emergency treatment of victims. The Mathematics in Information Technology and Complex Systems (MITACS) network works with companies in all sectors to help them adopt mathematical tools in their business. The Auto 21 NCE deals with passenger safety, with new materials and manufacturing methods, with energy efficiency and clean combustion of alternative fuels, with the regulatory domain, and much more.

The NCEs have become a proven source of solutions in very complicated problem areas and of highly-qualified people (HQP) able to follow up. They also have the mandate and capacity to commercialize any IP emerging from their work that might have innovation potential. Perhaps the most sincere praise for the NCE program is the recent appearance of some very similar programs in the EU and elsewhere around the world.

The NCEs and 4th Pillars are institutional innovations that Canadians developed to meet the need for critical masses of competence in important areas in a huge and thinly populated country. In a physical sense they are virtual institutions whose members and facilities are distributed across the land. But in the intellectual sense they are very real and strongly connected. Both of them must be counted among Canada's strategic assets, as we work toward a more prosperous future.

NOTES:

1   On page A11, in continuation of a front-page story.

2   We have a difference in usage here. In this book, products are taken to include both goods and services, but in the third bullet in the *Wall Street Journal* box "product" clearly means a good or an artifact.

3   The classic "Innovation, The Attacker's Advantage" by Richard Foster, McKinsey (1986) describes how to decide when to stop investing in improving a product and move on to developing a new one, and foreshadows some of the ideas later developed by Christensen. "Innovator's Dilemma" by Clayton M. Christensen, Harvard (1997) discusses disruptive vs. sustaining innovations through case studies from various sectors. "Dealing with Darwin" by Geoffrey A. Moore, Portfolio (2005) describes how great companies innovate at every phase of their evolution.

4   Report on Canada's Industrial Performance, Second Half of 2006, Micro-Economic Policy Analysis Branch, Industry Canada—downloaded from the Strategis website, July 2007.

5   Statistics Canada, CANSIM tables 376-0001 and 376-0002, accessed from the Statistics Canada website July 13, 2007.

6   "National Systems of Innovation: A Research Paper on Innovation and Innovation Systems in Canada," National Research

Council of Canada, Corporate Planning and Evaluation, April 1994, 78 pages. David Griller and le Groupe SECOR Inc. did the research, summarized on p. 28.

7   Those produced only for the domestic market.

8   2(product or process) x 3(manuf., service to business, service to home) x 3(world-first, Canada-first, company-first) x 4(science based, craft shop, systems integrator, technology purchaser) = 72.

9   Small and medium enterprises; see note 13.

10   The Canadian Oxford Dictionary, Oxford University Press Canada, 1998. The same thing is put slightly differently in the table of definitions later in the chapter.

11   The word technology is often very loosely used, provoking not entirely frivolous quips such as "The First Law of Technology Transfer is that first there must be technology."

12   "Science and Technology Data—2005," Industry Canada, Policy Branch, March 2007.

13   "Canadian Industry Statistics," Industry Canada, Strategis website, accessed July 19, 2007. Large establishments have more than 500 employees; medium establishments have 100 to 499, small ones from 5 to 99.

14   T. A. Brzustowski, "Innovation in Canada: Learning from the Top 100 R&D Spenders," Optimum Online, Vol. 36, Issue 4, December 2006.

15   John A. Schey, Introduction to Manufacturing Processes, 3rd ed. McGraw-Hill, Boston, 2000.

How University Research Helps

"Students are to ideas, as mosquitoes are to malaria."
—Guy Danielou[1]

I t is no coincidence that Canada stands second only to Germany at the top of the G-8 in the proportion of university research that is funded by industry. The numbers are 11% for Germany and 9% for Canada, both well ahead of the UK and US, which place next at 6%.[2]

This state of affairs may be surprising, since university-industry partnerships in science and engineering have a history of one and a half centuries in Germany and only about three decades in Canada. However, there are two good reasons for it. First, Canadian university research in science and engineering has achieved high quality, and the academic sector is therefore able to help solve challenging problems for which industry's own capacity is limited. Second, there are some excellent government-supported programs for university-industry research partnerships.

Three main ways

Canadian university research in science and engineering is very good. Its quality is high, and it is kept at world standards by a vigorous international peer-review system. Government investments over the last decade have provided a real boost by attracting talented new people and improving research infrastructure. Canadian researchers are not only good, but also productive. Looking again at the countries with the largest economies, which were compared in Chapter 1, Canada contains just 0.9% of their combined population but produces 4.7% of the world's research publications.[3]

But as already pointed out in Chapter 5, Canadians cannot be content to stay abreast of Canadian research; we must maintain our access to all the world's new knowledge. Today, having access to research results means not only being able to find the papers, download them from the Internet, and read them, but also being able to understand them, to assess the quality of the research, and to build on the new knowledge reported. To be able to do that, Canadian researchers must work in most of the areas of science and engineering in which advances are being made around the world; they must be good enough to understand what is being done by the world's best; and they must then make that knowledge available to industry. Fortunately, our researchers have been fulfilling all of these requirements, and that makes our 4.7% of world research an admission ticket to 100%.

All of this can also be said of health research in Canadian universities and research hospitals. The numbers might be somewhat different, but the conclusions are the same. Substantial differences arise only when we look at the ways in which university research is connected with wealth creation in the economy. We will come back to this point later.

Canadian university research in science and engineering contributes to wealth creation in our economy in three major ways. These differ in terms of the benefits to be derived form them, the time scale of their contributions, and the risks they involve.

How University Research Helps

The first way is through the education of students who become available for employment upon graduation. Students taught by professors who themselves do research are likely to be aware of modern developments. When hired by industry, they will learn quickly to work with new technologies. They might typically be ready to contribute after a year or less of further training on the job, possibly much less for co-op students[4] who previously worked for the same company. In terms of the company's innovation capacity, such people can most readily contribute to incremental innovation driven by market feedback, but their capabilities can be enhanced with the right experience. The greatest source of risk to the company could well be in the process of recruiting the right people in the first place, and then providing them with appropriate learning opportunities to develop their capabilities. All things considered, many people in industry believe this is by far the most important interaction between university research and wealth creation.

The second connection between university research and wealth creation in the economy is particularly well developed in Canada. This is project research done in partnership with industry. It is the kind of research that is undertaken when a company has defined a problem that needs solving but cannot be solved with existing knowledge, and when there is no capacity for generating the required knowledge in house. (If the required knowledge existed, the job of solving the problem would likely go to a consultant or a design shop.) Project research must meet two criteria to be useful: the research must be very good, and the project must be very well planned and managed. The benefits are twofold as well: first, a successful project may lead to significant process or product innovations that can be commercialized by the partner company, and second, the graduate students who worked on the research are potential employees who are already familiar with some of the company's technology challenges and ready to contribute right away. They expand the company's capacity for innovation by their capability to create and use new knowledge. The risk to the companies is also twofold but not unique to project research: first, the scientific risk always implicit in research, and second, the business risk of putting the results to use successfully. The benefit is obvious: potential commercial advantage from process and product innovations derived from new knowledge that is, at least initially, not available to competitors.

Thousands of Canadian companies of all sizes in all sectors have profited from such university-industry partnerships over the last two decades, and there are many successful federal and provincial programs that share the cost of such work (e.g., the federal Networks of Centres of Excellence and NSERC University-Industry programs, Ontario's Centres of Excellence, Alberta's iCORE). This is an area in which Canada has produced several very successful institutional innovations.

Two related additional interactions between university research and industry should be added here. Both depend on the expertise of faculty and their knowledge of industrial problems. They are research in areas of particular proprietary interest done under contract between a university and a company, and technical consulting by individual professors. Both contribute to industrial innovation.

The third major connection between university research and wealth creation is rare, unexpected, and difficult, but potentially very important. It is the occasional successful commercialization of some invention that arises out of the results of basic research—research undertaken only to deal with unanswered questions about nature. But because this process can often be identified with one person or a small group of researchers, because it can be serendipitous or dramatic (e.g., described in words such as "discovery," "breakthrough," and the classical "Eureka!"), and most of all because over the years it has produced some enormously important and well-known innovations that have had far-reaching effects on people's lives (e.g., the laser, nuclear fission, penicillin, etc.), it has become the focus of attention among policy makers, the media, and the public.

Some would say that the attention it gets is excessive but superficial, and that it leads to unrealistic expectations. In today's climate of (rightly) seeking fruitful outcomes for the expenditure of public funds, the question "What breakthroughs have you produced for the research money we gave you last year?" is not constructive. It overlooks the first two very important connections between university research and wealth creation discussed above, and it risks undermining the core process of basic research, namely the patient building up of a pyramid of facts from around the world to a major discovery at the apex. The challenge, of course, is to ensure that the apex is reached by Canadian researchers as often as possible.

That said, the Canadian record for commercializing inventions resulting from basic research is good. Given our low level of industrial R&D, in many cases there is no company that can pick up an unexpected invention and use it. This situation can be described as a low "receptor capacity" of Canadian industry for new research results. That means that in Canada the commercialization of inventions arising out of basic research often requires creating a new venture. Fortunately, we have learned to do that quite well, and we continue to get better at it. Canadian university research leads to more start-ups per dollar of research funding than in the US.[5] On the other hand, the revenue collected by universities from existing companies that license their inventions is much less than in the US, for the reason already mentioned.

Inventions coming out of basic research are already an important source of new ideas and of some innovations that change existing business to the point of being considered disruptive. But in the future they could become even more important. This is because many companies are withdrawing from long-term exploratory research under the market pressure to put more and more of their R&D money into faster and faster development of new products. In effect, industry is leaving long-term thinking to the universities.

The situation of health research in universities and research hospitals is different in many ways, but essentially the same in some others. It is different because the goal of health research is always to improve people's health. The new knowledge produced by research can lead to new ways of preventing illness, new tools for diagnosis, new medical instruments and procedures, new therapies, new drugs, new practice protocols, new rehabilitation regimes, new medical devices, etc. Some of these developments are very expensive, particularly because of the high cost of clinical trials, and when they are put to use the spending on health care increases. There is nothing unexpected in that, of course; our need to spend enough to provide good health care for an aging population is one reason why we have to increase and maintain our prosperity.

Nevertheless, health research in a university or hospital may occasionally lead to an invention that can be commercialized as a new good or service offered in the market. That creates wealth for the producers in the usual way, but if the new products are paid for out of tax revenues, the net effect is to consume more of the public wealth of the nation. However, if that product is marketed successfully in world markets, and the value-added industrial activity takes place in Canada, then we can say that health research has contributed not only to the well-being of Canadians but also to the country's wealth creation.

Canada is a relative newcomer to the world of research and wealth creation by science-based industries. As a result, we lack some of the key institutions that have evolved in many of the countries with which we compete, the various public and private institutions that routinely connect research with the market. As a result, we have much to learn, and we need to experiment with new arrangements and institutions designed with our particular needs in view. We have already produced some successful institutional innovations in the organization of research, but we need more. This means that more than just the scientific aspect of university research is important as Canada works to increase and sustain our prosperity in a fast-changing world. We also need competence and imagination in the organization and management of such research, and in the policies and agencies that support it.

The three ways in which Canadian university research in science and engineering interacts with industry are summarized in Table 7.1.

How the Canadian system works

In this section, we look at the organization of Canadian university research in science and engineering as a system. It's a complicated system, so we shall consider it in steps.

Figure 7.1 shows that the research is of two kinds: basic or project research, with some possibility of overlap. Research of

TABLE 7.1 The connections between university research in science and engineering and wealth creation in the economy

	Nature of the work done in industry	Time scale for effectiveness	Risk	Government role	IP implications
Hiring up-to-date graduates taught by researcher profs	Any R&D, e.g., for market-driven product improvement, as well as productivity-driven process innovation	From almost immediate to a year or two, depending on experience of students and company training capacity	Depends on recruiting skills—least risk with students out of co-op programs in research-intensive universities	None beyond providing research funding for the professors	IP issues are in the hands of the company
Partnership in university-industry research projects	Planned product or process innovation requiring entirely new knowledge that can't be generated in-house	Typically three to four years from defining the need to completing the project, may be longer if the company has no experience in dealing with universities	Scientific risk in doing the required research, and commercial risk in using the results effectively—latter can be reduced by hiring grad students who had worked on the project	Funding agency controls quality through peer review of both the proposed research and the project design, and provides part of the direct research cost	Government funds don't flow until the university and its industrial partner have signed an acceptable IP agreement
Commercialization of inventions arising out of basic research	Turning an unexpected invention coming out of basic research into a product and taking it to market, where it might prove to be an important radical or disruptive innovation	Several years, and could be longer if a start-up has to be created to turn the invention into a product in the market, and/or more research has to be done	Generally technology push, with high risk both in developing the new products and in the business aspects of bringing them to market	Funding agency controls quality through peer review of the proposed research, and provides the direct research cost	IP is owned either by the inventor or the university, according to university policy—IP may be licensed to an existing firm, or a start-up created to commercialize it

110

any kind is the process of learning what nobody yet knows. The only goal of basic research is discovery. Basic research is undertaken to discover answers to important unanswered questions about nature, humans, and humans in nature, and to generate new questions in the process. It generally takes the form of a long-term program of investigation that can change direction along the way, as new findings suggest new approaches.

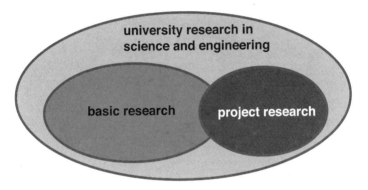

FIGURE 7.1   University research in science and engineering

Project research has already been introduced. This is research done when a practical problem—often but not always identified in industry—cannot be solved using existing knowledge. In that case, the research is organized as a planned project with specified objectives, a schedule, a detailed budget, a management structure, reporting of progress, and deliverables. Project research is generally carried out in a partnership formed by the university researchers and the industry people who defined the problem.

The conventional inputs and outputs of the research system are shown in Figure 7.2. The human inputs are those of the professors who act as Principal Investigators (PI) in the work, the graduate students who do the research as part of their programs of study for advanced degrees, the postdoctoral fellows who engage in research to raise their expertise to a higher level, and the research staff that support the work of all the others.

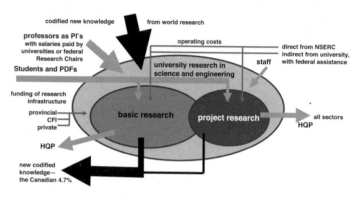

FIGURE 7.2 Conventional inputs and outputs of the research

The financial inputs are the necessary operating and capital funds. The direct costs of research are provided by agencies such as NSERC,[6] whose grants are awarded on the basis of peer-reviewed competitions. The indirect operating costs come through the universities with both federal and provincial assistance. The most important contribution of the universities to the operating costs of research, of course, is in the form of the salaries of the PIs.[7] The capital funds come from the general support of the universities by the provinces, from private gifts, and from other university sources. Specialized research infrastructure has been much improved in the last decade by peer-reviewed grants from the Canada Foundation for Innovation (CFI) that leverage both provincial and private matching.

The remaining input to the system is the flow of new knowledge from research done around the world, mainly in the form of codified knowledge in publications.

Two outputs from the research system are shown in Figure 7.2: new knowledge and highly qualified people (HQP). The new knowledge is in the form of publications that emerge mainly from basic research, with some contribution from project research. The HQP are educated in either basic or project research, with the latter group more likely (at least initially) to find employment in industry.

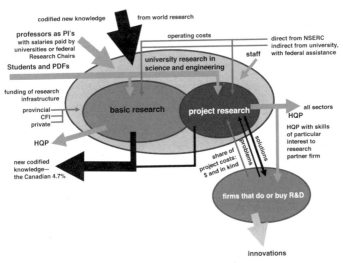

FIGURE 7.3   The Canadian system, showing industrial partnerships

A relationship that adds two more inputs and a third output is shown in Figure 7.3. This is the main reason why Canada compares so well with Germany in industry's support of university research. Companies that either do R&D themselves or buy it enter into university-industry partnerships for project research. They bring the research problems and pay a share of the project cost in cash and in kind. In return, they first get the quality control of peer review before they spend any money, and then if the project proposal competes successfully, they leverage some government funding. At the end of the project, they get the solutions to their problems and the opportunity to hire the HQP who were involved in solving them. Important innovations that follow are commercialized by the partner companies. Such relationships are supported by many government programs and agencies, for example, NSERC through its Research Partnership Programs (RPP), the Networks of Centres of Excellence (NCE), and the Ontario Centres of Excellence (OCE).

An additional output from the research system is shown in Figure 7.4. It is the potential intellectual property (IP) that sometimes emerges from basic research. If it appears to have innovation potential, the first stages of commercialization take place in the university, and the results either are licensed to an existing company or become the basis of a new venture. Any resulting innovations would then come from the licence holder in the first case, and from the start-up in the second.

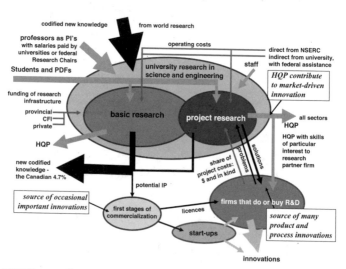

FIGURE 7.4   The Canadian system, showing potential IP from basic research

Three key parts of the research system have been labelled in Figure 7.4 (italics in boxes) to show the three different kinds of contributions to innovation and where in the system they come from. They correspond to the three rows of Table 7.1.

Commercializing inventions coming out of basic research

The commercialization of inventions coming out of basic research is the object of so much attention that it needs to be discussed in greater detail here.

Commercialization is the core activity of business, but in recent debates and policy discussions about the returns on the public investments in research, it seems to have been given a much narrower meaning. There is much talk about the "commercialization of research," an ambiguous phrase as it stands, but actually used as shorthand denoting the commercialization of inventions that emerge from the results of basic research.

Commercializing inventions coming out of basic research is not an easy thing to do. Two difficulties are fundamental. First, an invention arising out of basic research is an unexpected outcome of a process set up to do something entirely different: to help answer one of the unanswered questions about nature. And second, the unexpected invention is then promoted by the inventor who must claim "I've got a great idea!," which is very different from satisfying a customer who says "Help me. I've got a great need." In other words, such commercialization is driven by technology push, not market pull.

Figure 7.5 provides a more detailed description of the process of commercializing an invention derived from the results of basic research. This diagram is different in shape from Figure 7.4 but closely related to the last part added to it. Note that the

115

"potential IP" is identified by a downward arrow near the bottom of Figure 7.4 and by an upward arrow in the lower right corner of Figure 7.5. Following that arrow in Figure 7.5 takes one through what is labelled "first stages in commercialization" in 7.4.

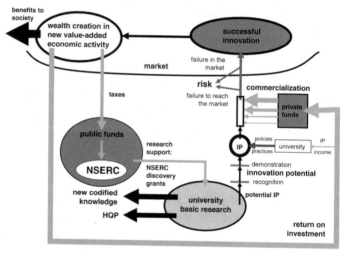

FIGURE 7.5 How a successful innovation can arise out of <u>basic</u> university research

The diagram shows commercialization by way of a new venture. To keep the diagram as simple as possible, the many false starts, dead ends, and feedback loops in the commercialization process are all hidden in the narrow vertical rectangle that swallows the IP, feeds on many stages of investment, and eventually produces an innovation.

Conventional wisdom has it that the cost of commercialization greatly exceeds the cost of the research that produced the invention.[8] It might range from a low of several hundred thousand dollars for a piece of software to billions of dollars for a new pharmaceutical. The diagram as a whole shows that a research grant to the right person in the right place at the right time can produce an innovation that succeeds in the market, meets needs that had gone unmet, creates new value-added economic activity that pays wages and taxes, and provides good returns for investors. When everything works, a small amount of public money can trigger a huge flow of private capital into the economy. Moreover, the public funds that are given for research are exposed only to scientific risk, and that is kept low by peer review. The private funds invested in commercialization are exposed to commercial risk: that of failing to reach the market or failing to succeed in the market for a whole host of reasons that may have very little to do with the merits of the innovation itself. In light of this reality, it cannot be said that this process takes something that the public has paid for and gives it away to business.[9]

The bottlenecks in this process are people and money. It's not enough to make an important discovery. It's not even enough to propose an invention on the basis of that discovery. Somebody who understands the science and knows the potential market has to recognize the innovation potential of what is proposed and to demonstrate it to people with money to invest. Then the money must come at the right time and in the right amount, and the investor(s) must have enough patience to give the innovation a fair chance to penetrate the market. And the whole process has to be managed by someone who is expert in the business of managing innovation and commercializing new products. We could use many more of all these people.

Commercializing the results of basic research performed in government laboratories would be generally similar to the process in universities, but differing in detail as a result of the mandates of the government departments housing the labs and their IP policies. In addition, there are substantial differences in the terms of employment of government scientists and university professors, and in the ways their research is funded. And, of course, another big difference is the involvement in university research of graduate students working for advanced degrees, which has no counterpart in government laboratories.

How do we measure success in the commercialization of inventions derived from university research? One indicator that is widely used by the universities is their income from licensing their IP. This is shown as the thin horizontal arrow running to the left from halfway up the right side of Figure 7.5. That income has been increasing in the last few years and now stands at over $50 million per year for all Canadian universities. However, there is a cost to managing IP, and the universities have been spending about $35 million on that. The net income is, therefore, a tiny fraction of the $25 billion total cost of the Canadian university system. So if the goal of commercialization is to develop a new source of university income, then success has been very limited.

However, I believe that the goal of commercializing inventions arising out of publicly-funded research is different, and on that different scale the success is already substantial. Consider figure 7.5 again, and particularly note the bubble at the upper left: "wealth creation in new value-added economic activity." This is what really matters; the IP income to the universities is incidental. According to Denzel Doyle,[10] the IP income to the universities is only about 2.5% of the new sales generated by products based on it.[11] That means that the university IP has generated about $2 billion in annual sales in the economy. That's a very significant number. It is about 2.5 times the amount that NSERC distributes annually in all of its research grants.

Nobody denies that the universities could use additional income, and use it very well. However, I believe that setting our sights on growing value-added economic activity would be more important in improving the system. Increasing the amount of the new economic activity would be the goal; increases in university income from IP would be incidental. This would entail making technology transfer as user-friendly as possible in order to get the university IP as quickly as possible into the hands of those who could use it to create wealth in Canada. The universities would get eventual returns through the tax system; but more immediate benefits might come if industry found the new approach so attractive that it started putting some returns directly back into the universities to keep new ideas flowing.

Canada's performance in innovation will not be improved by expecting researchers to become experts at commercialization. Good researchers should be supported to become the best researchers they can be. Commercialization requires expertise of a very different kind, and if we don't have enough experts in the business of commercialization and managing innovation, then that's the shortcoming on which to focus.

We must also remember that commercialization means different things to different people. Commercialization is the preoccupation of every entrepreneur; it is the essential function of all industry; but it is only an afterthought for the relatively uncommon researcher who is concerned with it at all.

Community colleges

While the universities have the major role in research-based innovation, another post-secondary entity, the community college system, has an important role to play in innovation that arises much more from current practice and market feedback.

Canada's 150 community colleges have campuses in almost 1,000 communities and provide a local technical resource to many small companies. This makes for a good match because most such companies don't engage in activities arising from research.

Most community colleges do not do research as such, although some would claim to be active in "applied research," an arguably vague description of their activities. However, it is much more important to recognize that community colleges can provide very valuable technical services to local companies, particularly small ones. Community colleges back up the business and technical resources of local small and medium enterprises (SMEs), helping them to solve production problems; adopt and adapt new technologies; design, build, and test prototypes; and develop market intelligence and business plans. When measured by appropriate standards, the best colleges are excellent resources for supporting innovation in business and industry.

However, there is one other area where the importance of what the colleges can do seems not to be recognized widely enough. This has to do with training. It is well known that community colleges provide many accredited diploma programs. In this they offer supply-driven education, as do the universities. They set the entrance requirements, the course content and emphasis, the format, schedule, location, duration, and graduation requirements. The supplier calls the tune.

But that's not all the colleges do. They also offer demand-driven training. They develop and offer programs tailored to meet the needs of specific employers and groups (e.g., "I've got seven electrical technicians here who need a course in LED lighting controls. They're available at the plant for two hours on Thursday afternoons for six weeks starting Thanksgiving. Your Mr. Jones has helped us in the past, and I think he would know exactly what they need. Please give me a proposal by next Friday"). The personal expertise of college faculty does not necessarily limit the range of the training the colleges can provide. They are perfectly able to find and hire university professors part-time to fill out their offerings. It seems to me that the performance of Canadian business and industry in worker training could be much improved if demand-driven training provided by community colleges were much more widely used.

If the designation "centres of excellence" is fitting for concentrations of what the universities do best, then the designation "centres of expertise" might be equally appropriate for concentrations of what the community colleges do best.

Government laboratories

Government science, in Canada mainly a function of the federal government, is an important activity in the economy. An industrialized economy needs certain elements of knowledge infrastructure that only the public sector can provide: standards and codes; specialized facilities that industry needs but no single company can afford; windows on emerging areas of science and high-risk technologies; research to provide the basis of public policy in many areas; a range of research, monitoring, and response capabilities in various areas of public safety; research supporting regulatory functions; long-term cataloguing of natural resources; research to understand natural hazards and turn them into manageable risks; rapid response capability in the investigation of accidents of many kinds; services such as weather forecasting and national statistics; and much more.

There is no wholesale connection between these activities and wealth creation, but many different and important connections exist in specific areas. But has the whole enterprise been looked at as a system meeting the country's needs? Do we have all the government science that we should have, or are there gaps to be filled? Are we still doing things we no longer need to do? Is the science of the necessary quality? Are its results accessible to all those who need them? Could some of it be done better in other places than those currently used, or in other organizations? Will the science establishment be in good shape tomorrow? Is it being renewed by new people with new ideas? Such important questions are just now starting to be asked. We should hope for thoughtful and comprehensive answers that relate government science to raising Canada's prosperity and improving the quality of life of Canadians.

NOTES:

1   President of the Université de technologie de Compiègne, at convocation at the University of Waterloo in 1982.

2   "Science and Technology Data—2004," Innovation Policy Branch, Industry Canada, March 2006. The data in this case are for 2002. The high for all countries in that year was China at 35.9%.

3   "Science and Technology Data—2005," Innovation Policy Branch, Industry Canada, March 2007. The data refer to publications in all fields by researchers in all sectors. If the populations of India, China, and Brazil, are left out of this comparison, then Canada produces about 4.7% of the papers with 2.8% of the population.

4   Many universities in Canada offer co-operative education, in which students alternate between study terms on campus and jobs in industry. For example, the University of Waterloo operates in the co-op format in most of its programs, and

has the world's largest co-op enrolment. Industry considers these students particularly valuable because they already know a lot about work in industry when they graduate.

5   Bruce P. Clayman, then V-P, research of Simon Fraser University, studies of university technology transfer and commercialization for the Canada Foundation on Innovation, 1998-2000.

6   Natural Sciences and Engineering Research Council of Canada, the federal agency that supports university research in science and engineering.

7   A rough but useful indication of the university contribution of this form is the "1/3-1/3-1/3 rule," namely that university professors spend 1/3 of their time in each of teaching, research, and other service.

8   T. A. Brzustowski, "Innovation = Invention + Commercialization: A Systems Perspective, Optimum Online, Vol. 36, Issue 3, Sept. 2006, pp. 1-8.

9   A criticism frequently levelled in the 1990s at attempts to expand the commercialization of inventions emerging from the results of publicly-funded, basic research in Canadian universities.

10 Denzel Doyle, "Cost recovery from publicly funded research," Opinion Leader, *RE$EARCH Money*, Vol. 21, No. 1, January 18, 2007.

11 My own estimate, see Note 8 above, is more conservative at about 5%, a number close to the proportion of sales revenue spent on R&D by Canada's Top 100 R&D performers.

Improving Things

"After all is said and done,
much more has been said than done." —Bob Rae

The quotation with which I ended Chapter 1 has angered me for years, because it's too close to the truth. It makes me think of the Avro Jetliner, the Avro Arrow, the vertical wind turbine, Telidon computer graphics, the Bras d'Or hydrofoil, and other examples of Canadian inventions that might have become major innovations in the fields with which I am familiar. For various reasons, they were abandoned, and the opportunities were left to others to exploit. And I know that other people have their own lists of Canada's missed opportunities in other fields. But anger can be motivating. Because of that comment, I decided to learn why Canadians often fail to realize the commercial benefits of inventions that our excellent science and engineering make possible, and to try to improve things.

The concern with Canada's innovation performance is widely shared. Over the years, roundtables, think tanks, expert panels, committees, organizations, and institutions in the public and private sectors have studied, discussed, and debated various aspects of this problem, and proposed improvements and new strategies. In this chapter, we will look at a small sample of such studies, two recent reports by the Canadian Manufacturers and Exporters, and by the Conference Board of Canada, as well as one not-so-recent one by the Ontario Premier's Council. We will conclude by comparing the Science and Technology Strategy recently published by the Government of Canada with earlier proposals.

CME 20/20

Canadian Manufacturers and Exporters (CME) is an association representing the interests of Canada's manufacturing industry in all sectors. In 2005, they published the results of a Canada-wide consultation called "20/20 Building Our Vision for the Future" (98 meetings across Canada with 2,500 manufacturers and stakeholders).[1] The consensus that emerged from this process was that "business as usual is not an option."

The 62 recommendations can also be interpreted as a list of the perceived needs of the established manufacturing industry in its current state. They are labeled "A Call to Action" and directed to ten target groups: "Canada's manufacturers"; "Workers and labour groups"; "Canada's school systems, colleges, universities, and training programs"; "Research centres and industrial assistance programs"; "Canada's business and financial services sector"; "Community leaders and economic development agencies"; "Local governments"; "Provincial governments"; "Canada's Federal Government"; and even "All Canadians," so nobody can feel left out. And for utter completeness' sake, the list also includes a commitment by CME itself to undertake 22 supportive actions. Manufacturing seems to be everybody's business.

The list of needs is long and comprehensive, and it's obvious that the CME consider all of them important. The calls to action are all imperatives, with most of the target groups being told that they "must" or "have to" do something. However, there is no indication of how these things are to be done, what the costs might be, and who is expected to pay. Nevertheless, the call for better support of Canadian manufacturing is too important to be left just as an exhortation, so it is a good thing that among its own 22 commitments, the CME includes some follow-up actions.

For the purposes of this book, it is enlightening to go through the CME list of the 62 needed actions and note any references to "productivity" and "innovation." There are surprisingly few direct ones, and the phrase "value-added" doesn't appear at all. Here are the two statements I consider most revealing:

Canada's manufacturers must:

Adopt Lean and other best practices to improve *productivity*, manage change, and sustain business growth;

Significantly increase investments in market-driven *innovation*, product design, engineering, and automation capabilities.

The introductory text about innovation is more informative. It underlines the gap between the perception of innovation by the manufacturing industry on the one hand, and how it is seen by the public sector and treated in public policy, on the other. To put it bluntly, and at the risk of some exaggeration, the manufacturing industry is interested only in sustaining innovation and improvements in the existing system; government and academia think only of disruptive innovation arising out of research. This gap may not be the major determinant of Canada's poor innovation performance, but it surely doesn't help to improve it.

This is how the CME makes its point[2]:

Innovation. Canadian manufacturers must be recognized as the benchmark of the world for innovation, flexibility, and continuous improvement. Innovation must be an integral part of business strategies aimed at managing change …. Innovation and continuous improvement must be priorities throughout manufacturers' supply chains…. Public support for innovation must be driven more by market opportunities for commercial application and less by research agendas or the goal of pushing technology into the marketplace. Research and development activities on the part of universities, colleges, and research centres must respond more effectively to the needs of manufacturers. Research centres must base their activities in areas of the country where they are closest to their industrial customers. And, stronger linkages are needed among manufacturers, universities, colleges and research centres…. Manufacturers need speedier and easier access to government support programs aimed at enhancing innovation, including the SR&ED tax credit system…. Finally, procurement by governments and public agencies must aim to promote the cost-effective development of new industrial technologies.

The contrast between these words and the "Porter Admonition" quoted in Chapter 5 is striking. What CME describes as a major thrust for the future, Porter describes as passé—the initial condition for change that competitive companies already take as a given.

But change must begin with the here and now. That means that the needs identified by the CME should be taken very seriously. And it turns out that the CME is not a lone voice.

Six quick hits for Canadian commercialization[3]

The Conference board of Canada (COBC) has long had an interest in the country's economic performance. An important series of annual diagnostic reports entitled "Performance and Potential"[4] has been identifying many aspects of the problem. A major, recent four-volume study under the title "The Canada Project—Mission Possible"[5] has dealt exhaustively with many of the issues raised in this book. A recent study entitled "A Report Card on Canada"[6] is another important source of relevant material.

"Six Quick Hits" describes six very specific changes that could improve Canada's innovation performance in the short term. These are the recommendations of the "Leaders' Roundtable on Commercialization," a group of 47 senior people from government, business, and academia including myself in an earlier capacity. They are as follows:

- **Industry-led Collaborative Research Networks (ICRN):** *"The goal of this quick hit is to establish collaborative research networks that bring together suppliers, research labs and anchor businesses to improve the level of innovation in supply chains."* The idea makes eminent sense and is based on the Beacon Project initiated between General Motors of Canada and the universities—including, significantly, the new University of Ontario Institute of Technology (UOIT). That means that the lessons being learned in the Beacon Project are already available to guide the creation of other such networks. However, the language describing the ICRN is surprising for its total lack of reference to engineering. Design, development, and testing will undoubtedly prove to be important in the work of these networks, and engineers are the technical people leading those activities. It is my impression in reading many Canadian reports that they show a lack of understanding about what engineers do in the economy. We can only hope that this lack is limited to the people who write the reports.

- **Regionally-based Commercialization Internships:** This proposal is intended to address the country's *"paucity of skilled and experienced entrepreneurs capable of transforming new ideas into products and services that customers want."* The proposed remedy for this is to expand the existing and very successful activities of the WestLink Innovation Network. I believe that the need is serious, and that the proposal would work because WestLink has a proven approach.

- **Angel Tax Credits:** The goal of this proposal is to make it easier for entrepreneurs to find risk capital in Canada, particularly in amounts less than $5 million. The mechanism is a tax credit for angel investors who would provide seed financing, as proposed by the National Angel Organization (NAO). This is a well-reasoned and compelling proposal because it can deal with two of the entrepreneur's most important needs at one time. *"The most effective source of seed financing is the individual who has invested before and understands the risks: the angel investor. The Canadian population of angels is very small—particularly when compared to that of the United States. We need to establish effective tax incentives that will attract more investors to the angel community. **Entrepreneurs rely not only on angel investment—early-stage high-risk capital—but they rely also on the mentoring, knowledge and experience that angels bring with them.**"* [emphasis in the original]

- **Pilot Program to Expand R&D Tax Credits:** The goal of this proposal is both clear and important: *"... a pilot program should be established to enhance the effectiveness of the Scientific*

Research and Experimental Development (SR&ED) tax credit by including corporate expenses related to the broader innovation process, not just to R&D.... The pilot program will test the expansion of the tax credit to include market assessment activities...." Obtaining market intelligence is the first such activity that comes to mind. Given the importance of speed in innovation, as already discussed in Chapter 5, market intelligence must not only be thorough but, to be useful, must also be kept up to date. While the network of Canadian trade and technology representatives in our embassies and consulates abroad can be helpful, detailed market intelligence associated with the possible introduction of new products is best left to companies, and money spent in obtaining it is an important part of the cost of commercialization. The SR&ED program is a known quantity, and the proposed pilot program could lead to an important improvement in its effectiveness.

- **Strategic Procurement:** This is a good proposal for good reasons. *"Governments and large businesses can drive commercialization through the purchase of leading-edge Canadian technologies.... Yet we seem to have lost the ability to use government expenditures as a way to help Canadian companies build the experience they need to become strong contenders in the global markets."* It is not only embarrassing, but may be fatal in marketing new Canadian products abroad, if the Canadian vendors must admit that their own government and big businesses are not customers. At its best, strategic procurement by government exerts a market pull that can promote the development of new technologies in useful forms, and at the same time share the financial risks involved. This is not about "picking winners," an expression used too often with too little regard for its appropriateness. It is about encouraging Canadian industry to meet the needs of its government for goods and services with new products that would be better than anything available from anywhere else, and then encouraging them to sell those new products in global markets.

- **Federal Seed Capital Investment:** This quick hit proposal differs from the others, in that it deals with more effective management of funds already committed. The Government of Canada had committed seed capital funds to be managed through the Business Development Bank of Canada (BDC). In the words of the proposal, the quick hit is that *"These funds should be used to lever private funds and attract* **experienced** *venture capitalists who can provide financing, insight and mentoring to Canadian businesses"* [emphasis in the original]. While the language of this recommendation is not direct, it is clear that as of the time of writing the quick hits (April 2005), the BDC had not moved as far as hoped in leveraging the federal government's money, and the Round-table was prepared to offer its help to both the government and BDC to speed things up. At the time of this writing (August 2007), it is difficult to find the numbers to judge progress, but an important condition for success is in place. The website of BDC shows that Technology Seed Investments, a dedicated business unit founded in 2002 and referred to in the quick hit proposal, has a management team of nine executives with impressive educational credentials and relevant business experience.

It is clear that quick hits 1, 4, and 5 echo the call of the CME. The remainder, 2, 3, and 6 deal with starting new ventures. But there's nothing new under the sun ...

The Ontario Premier's Council

The Ontario Premier's Council was a multi-sector advisory body set up by Premier David Peterson in 1986 to *"steer Ontario into the forefront of economic leadership and technological innovation."* There were 22 members from business, labour, and the universities, as well as six Cabinet ministers. The Chair was the Premier himself, and the secretary was the Deputy Minister of Industry, Trade, and Technology. The Council's first report came out in 1988.[7]

The objectives of the Council are worth stating in full because they are just as important and current today as they were 20 years ago.

Ontario should:

- Encourage all industries to move to competitive higher value-added per employee activities which can contribute to greater provincial wealth.
- Focus industrial assistance efforts on businesses and industries in internationally traded sectors.
- Emphasize the growth of major indigenous Ontario companies of world scale in those traded sectors.
- Create an entrepreneurial, risk-taking culture that fosters an above-average number of successful start-ups in internationally traded sectors.
- Build a strong science and technology infrastructure which can support the technological needs of our industries.
- Improve the education, training, and labour adjustment infrastructure to levels adequate to sustain the province's industrial competitiveness and help workers weather the technological change and adjustment necessary to move to higher value-added per employee activities.

- Follow a consensus approach, like that embodied in the Premier's Council, in the creation of both economic strategies and specific programs and in the mobilization of public support for the new directions.

Twenty years later, these are still pressing objectives.

Fourteen recommendations for follow-up actions were developed by the Council. Five of them were financial, recommending the creation of new incentives for: recapitalization of Ontario companies in traded sectors; increasing R&D expenses; risk sharing in new projects; early-stage VC investments; and IPO. Five dealt with various people issues: worker adjustment; worker ownership; technical personnel assistance for SMEs; education, training, and labour market policies; and excellence awards to individuals. One dealt with industrial restructuring in the traded sectors, one with redirecting government research to industry, and one with setting up a program for strategic procurement. Again!

The remaining recommendation to refocus the Ontario Development Corporations (regional development agencies) is reproduced below since it captures several themes that many might consider as national priorities today.

The Government should accelerate the refocusing of the Ontario Development Corporations according to the competitive priorities identified in this report. Specifically, this will require adjusting the ODCs' own priorities to:

- Provide assistance only to businesses in manufacturing and tradable services sectors.

- Build an active relationship with successful middle-sized companies and assist these firms to make the leap into world export markets.

- Improve ODC response times for reviewing and processing applications to match the best industry standards.

- Assist the development of Ontario's high growth industries by providing needed funds for prototype development and marketing as opposed to emphasizing fixed asset lending.

- Orient all assistance to encourage companies to move to higher-value-added products.

- Emphasize these strategic priorities even when pursuing regional development objectives.

A second report, "People And Skills in the New Global Economy,"[8] dealt with education for the new millennium, the deficit in worker training, and adjusting to change. It included 32 recommendations. As it happened, however, the Peterson Government was defeated in an early election, and the recommendations in the two reports were not implemented.

We now turn to Canada's recently published science and technology strategy to see what improvements are recommended there and how they compare with the three sets of proposals that we've just looked at.

The new federal S&T strategy

In May 2007, the Government of Canada published the S&T strategy[9] that had already been foreshadowed in an earlier economic plan[10] and reinforced in the most recent budget.[11]

My own reading of the main message behind the strategy is something like this: "Canadian university research has been raised to world class in many important areas, and we will invest to keep it there. But the country's economic performance is lagging because of weaknesses in commercialization by the private sector, and we will work with them to improve that."

The strategy is framed by three advantages: in knowledge, in people, and in entrepreneurship. The actions planned to achieve each of them are expressed as policy commitments. Some are quite specific as to how and when they will be funded and implemented; others are stated in general terms. Here is a list, in my own words, of those commitments that deal with some of the issues identified in the other reports discussed earlier in this chapter.

Focusing only on the entrepreneurial advantage, the government commitments are to:

- Make tax changes to help manufacturers invest in machinery and equipment;
- Improve the SR&ED tax credit program, including its administration;
- Create business-led research networks;
- Stimulate the supply of venture capital;
- Create new Centres of Excellence in Commercialization and Research;
- Fund community colleges to help small local businesses with technology.

But there is no mention of strategic procurement, even though the need for it has been identified by the three groups discussed above and many others as well.

The new program of Centres of Excellence in Commercialization and Research is important because it reveals a new approach. At one time, it seemed that government thought that the way to improve Canada's innovation performance was to make researchers into entrepreneurs. That would be resisted by most researchers, and it wouldn't work anyway, except for those few researchers who already happen to be natural entrepreneurs. The new program suggests that government now recognizes that commercialization of inventions arising from research can't be an afterthought. It requires expert knowledge and skills just as research does, but of a totally different kind. The researchers need to become the best researchers they can be, just as the entrepreneurs need to become the best at what they do. Working together, they have a better chance to create innovations from inventions based on research results. I believe that these innovations are more likely to be important if the research is in strategically important fields in the first place, and I see the new Centres as the place where researchers and entrepreneurs can learn to work together in precisely this fashion.

My final point deals with the policy commitment on managing the federal government's activities in science and technology. A new Science, Technology, and Innovation Council (STIC) is being created to advise the government on policy issues in S&T and to produce reports on Canada's performance. This new Council will report to the Minister of Industry. It replaces three earlier advisory bodies, one on S&T in general (ACST), one on the government's own science (CSTA), and one on biotechnology specifically (CBAC). I have great hopes for STIC. Its mandate is compelling, it has been given a strong chair[12] and its membership is impressive. But my expectations are less sanguine, because structurally STIC is the same as its predecessors, a body that produces advice to one minister, through one department, an arrangement that doesn't have a great record of making the advice influential. This issue is raised again in the final chapter of this book.

Last thoughts on improving things

We have seen in this chapter that over the years many committees, study groups, expert panels, roundtables, etc., have studied the challenges of improving Canada's innovation performance and made recommendations on how to meet them. They have studied the issues in depth and proposed new programs, better incentives, changes in taxation, etc. Their recommendations have much in common; many of them deal similarly with the same issues. But another thing they have in common—unfortunately—is that few of them have been acted on.

But even if they had been acted on, would such proposals be enough to make our prosperity sustainable for the future? Probably not. Most of the recommendations call for quantitative change to the status quo: lower the rate of this, increase the rate of that, expand the scope of something else, do some more of this and a bit less of that, etc. In effect, they propose some fine tuning of the current system. But our future will be qualitatively different from our present in many ways. And preparing for it must go far beyond improving what we do today. To do things very differently, and to do very different things, is difficult. It requires leadership and it requires learning.

We look at preparing for the future in the next, and last, chapter.

NOTES:

1   Canadian Manufacturers and Exporters, "20/20 Building Our Vision for the Future," a series of reports published by the CME with individual titles, including: "the Importance of Manufacturing in Canada" (2004); "Manufacturing Challenges in Canada" (2004); "The future of manufacturing in Canada—Perspectives and Recommendations on Workforce Capabilities" (2005); and "The Future of manufacturing in Canada—Executive Overview" (2005); no ISBN

numbers assigned, information available on the Internet at www.cme-mec.ca.

2   CME 20/20 Executive Overview, page 10.

3   "Six Quick Hits for Canadian Commercialization," The Conference Board of Canada, April 2005, ISBN 0-88763-680-02.

4   For example, "The World and Canada—Trends Reshaping Our Future," Performance and Potential 2005-06, The Conference Board of Canada, 2005, 183 pages, ISBN 0-88763-702-7.

5   "The Canada Project, Mission Possible," Volume I: "Stellar Canadian Performance in the Global Economy" (126 pages); Volume II: "A Canadian Resource Strategy for the Boom and Beyond" (132 pages); Volume III: "Successful Canadian Cities" (121 pages); Volume IV: "Executive Summary—Sustainable Prosperity for Canada" (59 pages), COBC 2007, ISBN 0-88763-737-X, -737-8, -739-6, and 746-9.

6   "How Canada Performs—A Report Card on Canada," COBC Report June 2007, 149 pages, ISBN 0-88763-779-5.

7   "Competing in the New Global Economy," Report of the Premier's Council, Volume 1, 249 pages, Queen's Printer for Ontario, 1988, ISBN 0-7729-4062-2.

8   "People and Skills in the New Global Economy," Report of the Premier's Council, 237 pages, Queen's Printer for Ontario, 1990, ISBN 0-7729-7320-2.

9   "Mobilizing Science and Technology to Canada's Advantage," Industry Canada 2007, 103 pages, ISBN 0-978-0-662-45155-6.

10 "Advantage Canada," 2006.

11 "Aspire to a Stronger, Safer, Better Canada," The Budget Plan 2007, Canada Department of Finance, March 19, 2007, 477 pages, ISBN 978-0-660-19711-1.

12 Professor Howard Alper of the University of Ottawa, an outstanding chemist and research administrator, and the inaugural winner of the Gerhard Herzberg Canada Gold Medal in Science and Engineering from NSERC, the country's top award for a research career characterized by both excellence and influence.

Preparing
for the Long Term

Qualitative change is the acid test of leadership.

Thus final chapter deals with preparing to achieve higher productivity and a greater prosperity for Canada, and to sustain it over the long term. More change is required, and much of it will be qualitative change. It will not be enough to do a little more of this and a little less of that, improve some things, and abandon a few others. We will have to do some important things very differently, and some new things that we've never done before and perhaps never even thought of. There will be much to learn, and the time to start is now.

Nine specific proposals for helpful change are discussed in this chapter. They are far from a complete list, of course, and others may emerge as more pressing. But I believe that even these few changes will be difficult, and they will test leaders in all sectors of this country, because qualitative change is the acid test of leadership.

In the previous chapter we focused on improving things. Such changes can be made over the short term because they are small changes in existing systems or because the required learning has already taken place. Now we must extend our time horizon from years to decades and consider something much more difficult. We must move beyond improving a familiar local environment to creating the conditions for Canadians to succeed in a changing global environment that is barely predictable today. The thesis of this chapter is that the best bet in the face of such uncertainty is to create supportive conditions for entrepreneurial people in Canada to succeed in seizing new opportunities.

To create those supportive conditions, I believe our country needs to decide where it is going and then prepare itself for getting there. What I mean is that Canada must develop a capacity for strategic thinking, planning, partnership, and action that builds on what we are able to do now but takes it to a significantly higher level. We need to develop the capacity for joint planning and concerted action between the private and public sectors. We need strategic coherence in the policies and programs of all orders of government. We need the capacity for investment for long-term growth. We need to develop and mobilize today's untapped human resources. We need up-to-date science and engineering of the highest quality. And we need business leaders with the vision and skills to put these factors together and create commercial success. But we don't yet have all the people, institutions, and processes necessary to achieve these things, so we will have to develop those first. And that work needs to be started now.

The nine specific initiatives for change proposed here are not a complete recipe; much more will be required. But I believe that success in these nine measures would add up to a big enhancement of our capacity to succeed in the future. These proposals do not primarily involve science or engineering, but they do involve scientists and engineers, as well as politicians, businessmen, labour leaders, educators, and many others in our society. They deal mainly with the human side of things: values, attitudes, culture, trust, institutions, organization, leadership, partnership, practices, and seeing ourselves objectively.

Here are the proposed measures. I shall describe them briefly in turn.

- Offering government programs as a system.
- Developing the capacity for joint government and business strategic planning.
- Defining opportunities strategically.
- Promoting a long-term approach to investing.
- Developing entrepreneurial managers.
- Developing our untapped human resources.
- Working to become a world marketing powerhouse.
- Growing "3-legged people"!
- Developing a new business model for Canada.

That eighth one sounds quirky, but bear with me. The quirky label may make an important idea easier to remember.

Offering government programs as a system

Like the governments of all industrialized countries, the Government of Canada and some provincial governments offer a multitude of financial support programs for various kinds of research and innovation that cannot succeed without public investment. In science and engineering, they cover many kinds of activities, ranging from small grants for basic research in the universities to big investments that share the risk of large development projects in industry. The best of these programs are very well designed and administered, and through multiple audits and evaluations they have proved effective in meeting the needs on which they are focused. But however good the individual programs might be, their impact could be improved if they were managed as a system.

As it is, there are valuable projects that can "fall between chairs." This can happen even if funding agencies are interested and money is available. It can happen when the project doesn't quite fit into the programs of any one agency, even if it touches upon the mandates of several. As well, the success of a project started under one program doesn't guarantee that its later stages will be funded under a successor program. Indeed, there may be a gap between programs, or there may be a dead end and no successor program at all.

To complicate matters further, the many separate agencies and departments through which the programs are offered have their own distinctive policies and practices. Those practices have grown more burdensome recently, particularly in their reporting requirements, under the praiseworthy pressure for full accountability in the spending of public funds. This can impose a significant administrative burden on applicants, and particularly on those who need to deal with more than one agency. In the case of small businesses, where both money and time are generally in short supply, the administrative burden may prove to be a deterrent to seeking support that might have made a big difference in the fortunes of the firm.

There are advantages to offering government support through multiple agencies. The main one is the ability for a narrowly-focused small agency to develop the specialized knowledge of a limited client group, to understand their particular needs, and to implement appropriate criteria of quality and measures of success for their activities. Another is the ability for a small agency to be nimble and discerning in response to changing needs of the clients and changing constraints on their own operation. These are valuable attributes that must be preserved. There is no need to gather the programs into one huge agency in order to operate them as a system.

In an ideal world, all government funding programs in a given area would fall under the umbrella of one policy, and the programs would be designed to have no gaps and no dead ends. The administrative requirements would be harmonized, perhaps by client sector, so that progress through the system would require an applicant to add new information to an existing file, not produce an entirely new submission at every stage. The individual agencies would be responsible for applying the criteria of quality and success that are appropriate to the activities that they support. Every agency and department would interpret the umbrella policy in the same way and play its assigned role in harmony with all its partner agencies. There would be no turf wars, and all would be peace, seamless service, humming efficiency, and uninterrupted progress toward national goals.

In the real world, however, harmonization of programs across the federal-provincial divide would be extremely difficult. Even within the federal government, the research and innovation funding system would require active monitoring and coordination from the centre of government, with financial allocation to the agencies serving as the irresistible control signal. This would require changes in the machinery of government, but I am sure that it could be done if the leadership were committed.

Developing the capacity for joint government and business strategic planning

The system just described would be essential for implementing a joint strategic economic action plan of the government and the private sector. But how would such a plan be created? At the moment, Canada does not have the institutional capacity for it, but many countries do, so there is no shortage of models for us to follow. There are successful models across the economic size spectrum from Finland to Japan, so the scale of the economy is not an issue.

I believe that what Canada needs is a joint economic strategy committee with members from the top levels of both government and the private sector, who have the authority both to negotiate a national strategy and to commit resources for action. Both are essential, since this is where major enabling national projects would be authorized. It is important that this strategic committee be a national body with the provinces represented at the table; but given the resources and jurisdictions involved, the federal government would undoubtedly need to play the lead role. I fully realize the political challenges of setting up such a body within our federal system, and I also realize that it wouldn't be all that easy for the private sector either. However, I will start off by believing that our political and business leaders could prove equal to the challenge of setting up a new institution for creating a comprehensive national economic strategy that links the Canadian economy with science. The alternative, namely dismissing the idea out of hand because it seems too difficult to try here, is to deny Canada an instrument that many of our competitors have been using to great advantage, and thus to make securing our prosperity that much more difficult.

This "Joint Science and Economy Strategic Committee" (JSC) would have to be harmonized with the financial and legislative agenda of government. It would need to be chaired by the Prime Minister personally and include the Minster of Finance among its members. Given the growing globalization of economic activity, the Ministers of Foreign Affairs and of International Trade should also be at the table. It would be critical that, in producing its economic strategy, the committee not become a conduit for end runs around regulations on human rights, environment, competition, and other areas that are also important to the Canadian public. This means that the ministers responsible for these areas must also be members. The provincial counterparts of some of these federal ministers, representing several provinces, should be members as well. To ensure that they really do represent the interests of their stakeholders effectively in the JSC, and to earn the public trust for doing so, these ministers would need to develop meaningful and effective processes of public consultation on the implications of the large dimensions of the strategies considered.

On the private-sector side, JSC should have as members several high-profile business leaders known for their excellence as strategic thinkers. There should also be some leaders of business and industry associations that have a policy mandate and funds for common pre-competitive activities and infrastructure investments. These people should have the authority to negotiate and to commit resources for projects at the strategic level. The committee could, of course, not deal with the competitive commercial activities of individual firms.

The JSC should not operate under the rule that members "leave their interests outside the door." These words have the reassuring sound of high principle, but they are totally inappropriate for a forum concerned with action. On the contrary, all members should bring their legitimate interests to the table, describe them openly and fully, and set about developing plans that would harmonize them and fulfill them to the greatest extent possible.

A small dedicated secretariat would be needed to support the JSC. It should be staffed by people who are capable of learning broadly and quickly, and communicating very well. These people would have the usual responsibilities for process and transactions, but their main value would be to assemble the strategic information required. This would include market intelligence, technology road maps, science assessments, and business due diligence, as appropriate. The practice of international peer review to establish the quality of major Canadian proposals would not be appropriate for the JSC for two reasons. First, the formative stages of a national strategy should be held close for competitive reasons. And second, the quality of the science in any proposal should be established as first rate by peer review at a lower level in order to make it to the JSC agenda.

The proposed JSC is very different from the advisory system now in place in the federal government. As indicated in the previous chapter, over the years, there have been many advisory committees and councils of one kind or another, involving scores of competent and committed people from outside government, set up to advise the various departments and agencies of the Government of Canada on issues related to science, technology, and the economy.[1] Some of these committees were nominally chaired by Ministers, and one[2] was set up with the Prime Minister as chair. But Ministers quickly drifted away from these committees, showing that they thought the "real" business of government lay somewhere else.

Advice, of course, need not be accepted. It can also be rejected or ignored. In this connection, the "arm's length" nature of the advisory committees doesn't just signal their independence and objectivity; it also hints at their distance from government and the low degree of likelihood that their advice will influence government action. And when the advice to government is to be made public—another feature that is principled and reassuring—it is absorbed into the priority-setting process of government communications, often introducing unpredictable delays. And finally, since the advice is directed to government and not produced within it, the government must have the opportunity to develop its own response before any action can be expected. This is a deliberate and cautious process that may involve new rounds of consultation. And that introduces another delay, stretching the whole process to the point where it might no longer be timely. The proposed JSC could not function like that. It must be decisive and prompt. It must have the authority to decide and to commit resources, with authority much like that of a Cabinet committee.

The final distinction to be made here is between the advisory process in science and technology, and the assessment process recently launched. The independent Council of Canadian Academies (CCA) assembles expert panels to provide objective assessments of the state of knowledge in areas where scientific issues loom large, including some areas identified by government. There is no issue here of bringing interests to the table or leaving them outside the room. The interest of the expert panels and of the CCA is to develop an accurate picture of scientific knowledge in the subject areas as it exists currently, free from any biases or vested interests. This process is new in Canada, but well established in the US and other countries, and it already seems to be working very well. It could be very helpful in the work of the JSC.

Defining opportunities strategically

The first reaction to this heading might be that this is all about SWOT analysis—the systematic study of Strengths, Weaknesses, Opportunities, and Threats. Such analysis is certainly part of the picture, but the stress here is on the "O." On the scale of national strategies, labels and slogans come easily, but the real opportunities behind them are not at all obvious and defining them takes serious work.

For example, it is easy to say, "Canada has the opportunity to be the green energy superpower." That claim conjures up reassuring images of towering new hydroelectric power dams, lines of windmills swishing along high ridges, tidal power generators along our coastline, waste biomass fermenting to produce ethanol, and hydrogen-powered cars softly exhaling steam in traffic. But what exactly is an energy superpower, and how does it become green? What advantages does Canada have for achieving that status? What existing capabilities could we build on to create economic opportunities under that label? What new capacities would have to be developed? What specific forms might those new opportunities take? What might be required to seize them, and what might be the consequences? What do we need to learn to answer these questions?

A recent project of the Canadian Academy of Engineering[3] provides an example of the nature and scale of the effort required. Their "Energy Pathways" project involved several dozen expert engineers working as volunteers for the better part of a year. Some two dozen energy pathways were examined in terms of the state of scientific knowledge, the extent of Canadian practical experience, and the capacity of Canadian industry to become involved in them on a commercial scale. The outcome is a list of several national projects dealing with, for example, electricity from renewable sources and energy storage, in-situ extraction of bitumen from the oil sands, and CO_2 sequestration underground. The national projects involve a mix of laboratory research, pilot-plant development, and very expensive field tests with commercial-scale equipment. They are programs for learning what is needed in the selected areas.

There is financial risk in them at every level, but particularly in the field tests.

If these national projects are funded and carried out successfully, only then will it become possible to define the "green energy superpower" opportunities in sufficient detail to guide investment decisions by government and industry. There is no reason to believe that the energy domain is extraordinarily difficult to understand, so corresponding exploratory work is likely to be required to define new opportunities in other areas of the economy. In the system proposed above, I would expect JSC to commission such work, and to use the results in developing their strategies.

Promoting a long-term approach to investing

It has long been acknowledged that we in Canada are effective when it comes to creating good small companies but not very effective at growing them into good big companies.[4] Douglas Barber has pointed out in some of his recent speeches that the language of investment betrays an attitude that contributes to that state of affairs. Investors talk about "exit strategies" from successful ventures as soon as a good profit can be made rather than about staying to grow businesses over the long term.

We also have difficulties with public investments in existing infrastructure. It already exists and it still works, so there's not much news to be made by committing to keep it working for the long term. And if there is public praise to be earned, it could come only after several years, when some big project is completed or commissioned, possibly to the credit of some future government. And all the while, the government of the day feels political heat to spend more on solving urgent problems that are very much in the public eye at the moment. Investments in existing infrastructure become urgent only when some incident, such as a massive bridge collapse, captures the public's attention.

There are related issues with current spending on certain preventive measures. In the health area, people generally understand the risks of failing to adopt such measures, so vaccination and inoculation programs are supported. Money is quickly found to build up stocks of flu vaccine against a possible pandemic. Earthquake damage is understood because of TV news coverage of incidents in even the most remote corners of the world. Here again, investments routinely do flow as a result of appropriate updates to the building code and mandates for their application in new construction projects, as well as in some retrofitting and reinforcing of old structures in vulnerable zones. But, even though the death toll among drivers on our existing highways is staggering in comparison with incidents of bridge collapse, outbreaks of disease, or earthquakes, we do not invest enough in making the roads safer. The required knowledge and technology exist and are well proven, but the public and governments are inured to the risks inherent in the very familiar and widespread activity of driving on our roads.

And things get even more difficult when we enter the area of social programs designed to promote the development of children into competent adults. Such programs are another prevention measure; they decrease the future economic and social burden on society of caring for its adult members who cannot make it on their own. However, this area is always the subject of difficult debate involving cultural norms, political ideology, religious values, and organized interests, in addition to potentially high costs.

These issues affecting long-term investment are so complex that I shall make only two modest proposals here.

First, in the case of new ventures, I would urge changes in tax rules designed to provide an incentive for the investor to stay in new venture for a long time. For example, the federal government might consider a time-dependent tax rate for capital gains deriving from equity in a new Canadian venture. The rate could be very high, perhaps even 100%, for investments held less than one year, and could decrease with time, dropping to zero for capital gains on investments held for 10 years or more. Undoubtedly, tax experts in government could come up with other possible incentives of this sort. The main point is that incentives need to be devised to encourage investors to stay with small successful Canadian companies and help them grow into large ones.

The second proposal deals with investing in preventive measures. I think the academic community, the insurance industry, and the government could make an important contribution if they worked together to develop a widely understood and generally accepted approach to making the business case for investing in preventive measures of all kinds. This work should certainly involve economists, demographers, accountants, actuaries, and finance experts in government. Having a business case produced by generally acceptable methods will not dictate the decision on a particular investment, but at least it will provide estimated costs and benefits that are reliable and comparable with other investments.

Developing entrepreneurial managers

As I have used the term, entrepreneurial managers are those who are always seeking new ways to add value in their business. What sort of people might they be, and how could we develop more of them?

First of all, these are managers. They have already attained a position of some authority in an existing organization and are able to direct the work of others. They are proven performers. They are secure enough to "think out of the box," to promote innovations of all kinds. Some of those innovations might be their own ideas; others might come from any source inside or outside their organization. In all cases, however, the managers I call entrepreneurial have the capacity to visualize how these new ideas might be translated into new or improved products for the market, as well as to devise the business models for doing that. It is tempting to identify entrepreneurial managers with disruptive innovations, but that might be too simple. I can imagine entrepreneurial managers seizing opportunities for sustaining innovations that increase the value added in their company's existing product lines.

But they can't do it alone. The corporate culture in which they work must be supportive of innovation. If they are surrounded by signals that what matters most is improving the details of current activity, innovation is likely to suffer.[5]

Some people are naturally entrepreneurial. They become entrepreneurs on their own and will always be entrepreneurs, no matter what. But others may have latent entrepreneurial talent that needs the right opportunity to develop. I believe that education has a role to play in this. At best, this begins with imparting information, then moves to providing examples through case studies and by putting students in contact with active entrepreneurs, and ends by providing students with opportunities to be entrepreneurs themselves. This process can be started early. For example, for 25 years Canada's Shad Valley[6] program has been offering selected gifted high-school students four-week summer courses in science, technology, and entrepreneurship on

11 university campuses, followed by five weeks of co-op job experience in industry. Many of their 10,000 "alumni" have gone on to become technology entrepreneurs after their university studies. At a higher level, the MBET[7] program of the University of Waterloo provides students with a structured and assisted experience in taking to market the ideas that they have already been developing. In this area, as in so many others, we know what to do, and we do it very well; we just don't do enough of it.

And there are more things to try. For example, a special form of EMBA[8] might be developed that would have an important component of hands-on entrepreneurial experience for managers who feel that they have the potential to become entrepreneurial managers, and who work in companies that want to develop such capacities.

Developing entrepreneurial managers is an area where the education sector, working in close partnership with business, can make a big contribution for the long term. Since new educational programs take years to start up, and then years for students to complete, this work should begin now.

Developing our untapped human resources

Here I will focus on untapped human resources in just two groups of people: First Nations youth and immigrant professionals.

It has long been acknowledged that First Nations children and youth lead a hard life and face limited prospects for economic success as adults. Their high-school completion rates are only about 40%. But the data[9] also show that First Nations men and women who finish high school have the same chances of finding employment as other Canadians with the same level of education.

This finding suggests a concrete strategy to foster their development and improve their opportunities in life. The goal should be to raise that 40% much closer to 100. There isn't a ready recipe for doing that, of course. People have been working to increase First Nations high-school completion rates for a long time, but success has been limited and slow. However, I believe that there is a new urgency today, since success now will not only improve the economic prospects of First Nations people, but also improve the demographics of the entire labour force. I believe that a partnership of the First Nations, the Government of Canada, and the appropriate provincial governments and educational systems that was focused on this target, and given appropriate resources, could be capable of coming up with plans and actions that would greatly accelerate the increase in high-school completion rates of First Nations youth.

Success would improve the lives of future generations of First Nations people, but it would also have an economic impact on Canada as a whole. It could relieve some of the demographic pressure on Canada's workforce. In several parts of the country—Northern Ontario, Manitoba, Saskatchewan, and parts of Alberta—First Nations youth constitute the majority of young people. When they complete high school and whatever post-secondary education they choose, and then enter the workforce, they will provide it with some much-needed rejuvenation.

The other people that I consider an underdeveloped human resource are immigrant professionals. Canada is fortunate enough to attract many newcomers who have had a professional education in their home country. Unfortunately, however, far too many of them are prevented from practicing their professions in Canada. It is understandable that there should be caution about the quality of their credentials and the education behind them, particularly in professions that deal with aspects of public safety; but current practices often result in profound discouragement for the immigrants and a senseless loss of opportunity for the country. We simply must do better.

First of all, our assessment of professional education in the homelands of Canadian immigrants must be as thorough and up to date as possible. Many of these countries have recently been undergoing deep and rapid change, and the quality of the professional education they offer may be very different from what it was just a couple of decades ago.

Then, in the matter of ensuring adequate experience, we must learn to combine the two essential elements—Canadian testing for competence and supervised Canadian experience—in ways that are appropriate for educated professionals. This means that those who are qualified should be able to establish their credentials with minimum delay and begin to practice, and those whose qualifications need to be raised should be steered to the appropriate remedial training. And we shouldn't assume that the appropriate form of such remedial training must consist of sending people back through the corresponding Canadian professional curriculum. For many, this could be a major unnecessary expense and waste of time. We must develop the capacity to design remedial training programs that are more appropriate to the circumstances of the individuals.

In addition, the federal government must get its act together and develop policies and practices that are consistent among those officials who admit immigrants and those who assist in the job placement of residents. Somebody at a very senior level of the federal government must become accountable for doing this right.

Working to become a world marketing powerhouse

A visit to any university or college classroom in science, engineering, technology, or commerce quickly reveals that there are many students in the room who have "old country" connections with just about every country that Canada trades with, either by being immigrants themselves or through their families. Some of these students can speak the language of the old country, even if they were born in Canada. It seems to me that their presence could provide a strong foundation for developing Canada into a "world trade superpower."

This is very important, because value added depends on sale of the products. It is not enough to be strong in R&D and develop great technologies and new and exciting products. Those products must be sold. And given the limited size of Canada's domestic market, the success of Canadian value-added products in export markets is essential.

We have a million or so undergraduates in our colleges and universities. If just 0.1% of them, namely 1,000 students at any one time, spent one year of serious study in the old country, then Canada would gain 1,000 possible candidates per year for international marketing and trade careers. These people would have acquired some first-hand knowledge of the culture, economy, politics, environment, history, geography, business practices, and laws of at least one country. If this was done on a continuing basis, Canada's potential for great competence in world trade would grow significantly.

While there is nothing to prevent individual students from taking this path on their own, activity on the scale of thousands of students would have to be set up as a program. Two elements would be important. The first is financial. There would be a need to help students with travel costs, health care coverage, tuition fees, and the possible loss of income in foregone summer employment in Canada. The second is academic. Arrangements would have to be made for the year of study to count toward the participating students' degrees at their home universities. In the first instance, this would require bilateral institution-to-institution agreements, but if the scale were large enough that would become unwieldy and some simpler umbrella arrangement would have to be devised.

The number of 1,000 students per year seems large at first glance, but in reality it is quite modest. Canada has about 80 universities and some 150 community colleges, which means that on average only four students from each institution would be participating each year. At the level of particular institutions, one might easily find demand for much greater participation, perhaps many times greater.

It is not beyond imagining that there might be 10,000 young Canadians studying abroad in their families' old countries at any one time. It is hard to think of anything that could enhance Canada's reputation around the world more than a flood of energetic and motivated bright students, eager to learn and to establish connections with people in the lands where their own roots lie.

Nothing so far has been said about student exchanges, the most common format of programs for study abroad. I have treated this as a one-way, non-degree Canadian program designed for Canadian purposes that can be served without exchange. It requires a quick start, and its one-way flow prevents possible delays in arranging for symmetrical arrangements with other countries. But if exchanges of one-year, non-degree students could be arranged at a useful pace, the program would be even better. It would be good for Canada to welcome thousands of students into Canadian classrooms each year, help them learn about this country and its people, and build the foundations for various long-term, grassroots linkages between our countries.

Growing "3-legged people"!

I have given this section a quirky name to make the key idea more memorable. It is also a way of meeting the challenge of what to call—briefly—the people whose attributes I describe below. Perhaps readers will come up with a better name for them. If you do, please let me know.

It is generally recognized today that collaboration and partnership are the keys to the success of many organizations in this increasingly complex and interconnected world. In economic matters, collaborations among business, academia, and government have grown particularly important. But experience has shown that such partnerships are difficult to negotiate and not easy to maintain.

Partnerships are built on trust, and trust is easier to develop when people understand deeply the activities and goals of their potential partners. For that reason, I have come to believe that it is very important for nations to cultivate a number of individuals who have experience in leadership positions (CEO-level, or one level below) in all three sectors: business, academia, and government. Having played a major role in each, these people would know intimately the realities, values, pressures, and practices of all of three.

These "three-legged people," as I call them (because they have a foot in each of three sectors), could act as leaders in the creation of strategic, high-level partnerships among institutions and organizations in the three sectors. They would also be on hand to offer understanding and encouragement from the top of the organization when the inevitable difficulties showed up at the working level.

Vannevar Bush, quoted extensively in Chapter 3, was such a person. He was a professor of electrical engineering, dean, and vice-president at MIT. In government, he was a very senior public servant in Washington during World War II. The Manhattan Project reported to him. And in business, he was one of the founders of Raytheon Corp. He is perhaps the best known example of a "three-legged person" from the recent past, but there seem to be many other such people in the US today. Regrettably, very few such individuals come to mind in Canada, with the possible exception of one or two from Québec. Numerous other Canadians have had very senior experience in two of the three sectors, but not in all three.

Given the importance of such leaders, and the fact that they haven't been emerging spontaneously in Canada, I think we should set out consciously to develop them. One approach might be to identify those who already have the right experience in two sectors and work informally to develop attractive senior opportunities for them in the third. A small committee of very senior people from all three sectors would perhaps be the best group to take charge of getting that done.

Developing a new business model for Canada

We conclude with the most difficult and potentially the most important initiative. If approached in the right way, the process of developing a new business model for Canada could become a nation-building effort in participatory democracy; it could produce both sound ideas for making our prosperity sustainable and, at the same time, widespread public support for them.

Why a new business model for Canada?

In the economic sphere, a huge qualitative change affecting the whole world is the movement of the centre of industrial innovation. It has been moving westward since the middle of the eighteenth century and has now reached mainland Asia, where a third of the world's population resides. There it has the potential to expand enormously, with great implications for trade patterns around the world. Canada's economy is very dependent on trade, so we are bound to be affected.

The movement of the centre of industrial innovation is not a new process in the world, but I think that it has recently been accelerating. What I consider its current phase started with the publication between 1751 and 1776 in France of *L'Encyclopédie* of Diderot and d'Alembert. Among other things, that massive publishing project codified a vast compendium of the technologies of the day and made a lot of technological knowledge available beyond the guilds. I think of that process as analogous to a switch from a "trade secrets" model to the use of patents for protection of intellectual property.

From that point, the centre of industrial innovation moved across the English Channel to Britain, taking shape as what we now call the Industrial Revolution. Its best-known product was the steam engine, which led to the railway but also to steam-powered manufacturing machinery capable of producing high volumes of products.

The next hub of industrial innovation was the east coast of the US. In the late nineteenth century, this region produced a twofold legacy of mass manufacturing with interchangeable parts and, later, the electrical industry.

The next phase of innovation, the auto industry, took place mainly in the US mid-west. From there, the centre continued moving across the US to the west coast, producing jet travel and the digital revolution. Then it crossed the Pacific to Japan, where it produced an explosion of consumer electronics. Most recently it has moved to mainland Asia, which is beginning to look more and more like today's New World.

As the centre of industrial innovation moved west, the business models of the countries along the way evolved. Perhaps the biggest recent change has been the decline of manufacturing and the growth of services in the UK and North America, and the outsourcing of brand-name manufacturing and routine back-office services to contractors mainly in Asia. Even more recently, it is starting to affect the model of engineering education in the US.[10] There are now discussions about what new form US engineering education should take, given that not only manufacturing but also R&D and design are increasingly being outsourced to Asia by US industry. In what areas might future US engineers be able to maintain their advantage over their counterparts elsewhere? What will they have to do to keep earning their much higher standard of living? What changes in engineering education might be required to prepare them for that future? I am just starting to hear such questions being raised in Canada.

These considerations lead me to conclude that Canada must recognize this qualitative change and that an important expression of this recognition would be a new business model. Strictly speaking, we don't have an explicit business model. There seems to be an implicit one that I would describe as "the US with a time lag." The expressed short-term aspirations of leaders from government, universities, and some sectors of industry add up to a vision of a high-technology Canadian economy a lot like the US in the late 1990s but with little mention of services. Juxtaposed against that aspiration we have the unavoidable reality of a two-pronged exporting economy. One prong is in manufacturing, particularly transportation; the other is based largely in resources and in the supply of raw materials and commodity products to a world in which the competition is getting stronger and the customers more demanding. And services about which we talk little are already a big part of what we do.

This brings me to the process of developing a new business model for Canada. I believe that doing this could be very valuable, in terms of the results it could produce as well as the process of achieving them. I see it as an opportunity to launch a nation-building exercise in participatory democracy that would provide a strong basis of public support for whatever model emerged. Here are some of the most important features of the process:

The discussions should be very broad, involving governments, institutions, organizations, communities, and individuals.

The JSC would act as the Steering Committee, and there would be a small national secretariat backing up the process but no planeloads of civil servants arriving from Ottawa to organize it. All discussions would be organized locally, independently, in their own way and at their own expense, by communities, by local organizations, by governments, by neighbourhood associations, by volunteer groups, by institutions, by professional bodies—in brief, by anybody who wanted to put the effort into it.

All those interested in participating would receive the same document: a two-page summary of facts about Canada, and four questions. Their only responsibility to the Steering Committee would be to return the answers by a specified date and indicate whose answers they were and how they were arrived at. Institutional responses from the education, health, and municipal sectors should come back to JSC through the provinces; the rest may come back on-line or in some other direct way. However, I would rule out any cross-country tour of the JSC to receive presentations face to face. The number of such sessions would have to be limited to very few by time pressures on the JSC members, and that could be taken as suggesting that all the other submissions were less important. And even if the logistics could be managed in some miraculous fashion, the slim new insights obtained in this way would not justify the additional cost and delay involved. However, there would be nothing to prevent local groups or governments from organizing their own open sessions where many respondents could meet and discuss what they had submitted. The records of those discussions would contribute new value in the process.

The questions should be tailored in detail for the various groups participating, but they would all deal with the same four issues. For example, here is how they might be posed for discussions in a small town:

- What are your strengths, and the sources of wealth and prosperity in your community today?
- What do you expect your strengths and the sources of wealth to be in 10 years? In 20 years?
- What opportunities exist today for creating more wealth and making your community more prosperous, and what would it take for you to seize these opportunities?
- What new opportunities for producing more wealth and increasing prosperity does your community hope to create in the future, and what would you have to do today to make it possible to create them?

The accompanying fact sheet should deal realistically with the whole country and must not be just a box of bon-bons. It should be a tight but comprehensive list of strengths and weaknesses, as well as of challenges and achievements. Needless to say, some of the facts may be challenged or corrected in various places, but that would be a constructive feature. The nation-building aspect of this process is that all participants are made aware of problems and possibilities across the whole country, not just of their own. They then develop their own plans in the context of Canada as a whole.

Here is an example of what I have in mind:

- We are almost 33 million people responsible for a land mass of 10 million square km, but we occupy only a small fraction of that area—a strip along the southern border with the US.
- 80% of us live in cities.
- Manufacturing is a dwindling percentage of our economy but an anchor for many other activities. Services are growing, and most services originate in cities.
- 80% of our trade is with the US, and much of that has to squeeze through a small number of border crossings.
- We pride ourselves on our environmental consciousness but in fact pollute the air and water more than many other industrialized countries.
- Our production of commodities from natural resources consumes a lot of energy, produces a lot of pollution, and emits greenhouse gases, and all of these effects increase in proportion to the volume of commodities produced.
- Many Canadians are involved in a broad range of knowledge-based economic activities in which value is

added with minimal consumption of energy and very little pollution or greenhouse gas emission.

- We can no longer count on the cheap Canadian dollar to give our business a competitive advantage.
- The small percentage of us who live on farms have the potential, with today's technology, to be self-sufficient in energy; but we aren't because measures are not in place that would make the installation of the required systems affordable.
- Some of us still live in small company towns located close to concentrations of resources in remote areas, at a time when the producers in those towns are facing increasing pressure from global competitors whose products arrive at industrial centres by sea.
- We have a good education system, with strong participation at the post-secondary level.
- We have the world's longest coastline by far, but we have a small and obsolete navy, and our fisheries are severely depleted.
- Some of our largest and oldest corporations are no longer controlled by Canadians.
- We are very good at research and engineering, and at starting up new ventures, but we are less successful at growing these ventures into large, successful companies.
- We have some of the world's most beautiful natural areas protected as national parks.
- The mountain glaciers, permafrost, and Arctic ice are melting fast. This will have serious implications for water supplies to cities and for the northern habitat.
- We are good at managing very large engineering projects.

- Our claims to sovereignty over the Arctic are being challenged.

- We are very good in the domains of high technology and advanced manufacturing, and we can create leading-edge products of the highest quality in areas such as microsystems and robotics.

- We take pride in the performance of our health care system and its universal coverage, but complain about the delays in getting access to it.

- The railways, our main east-west link for the transportation of bulk goods, were built more than a century ago.

- Our cities have been shaped more by sprawl than by renewal.

- Most of us have become very dependent on the use of the car in our life and work.

- Many very talented Canadians choose to live and work in the US.

- We have enormous stores of natural resources, but we seem content to export them largely as raw materials and import some of them back as the value-added products of another nation's ingenuity.

- Our manufacturing workforce is capable of work of very high quality, and our publicly-funded health care system relieves our manufacturers of the long-term burden of funding health care plans for employees and retirees.

- We have an extraordinary multicultural society, which represents all the world's trading nations among us.

- We are very good at creating university-industry partnerships for research to solve practical problems in advanced industries and in other sectors.

If the process of developing a new business plan for Canada works really well, the result could be a much clearer view of the way ahead for Canada, with strong public support behind it.

NOTES:

1 The latest version of such a committee was announced in the spring of 2007.

2 The National Advisory Board on Science and Technology (NABST) was initially chaired by Prime Minister Mulroney.

3 Canadian Academy of Engineering, Energy Pathways Task Force, Phase 1 - Final Report, 63 pp., 2007, ISBN 978-0-9730830-3-3, also available electronically at www.acad-eng-gen.ca

4 For example, this was one of the issues examined in 1987 by the Premier's Council of Ontario in its study of what it would take to succeed in the new global economy.

5 Something like this happened at 3M, traditionally one of the world's great innovation powerhouses. See "3M's Innovation Crisis—How Six Sigma Almost Smothered Its Idea Culture," cover story in *Business Week*, June 11, 2007.

6 The Shad Valley program is operated by Shad Valley International. Details at http://www.shad.ca.

7 Master's in Business, Entrepreneurship, and Technology now offered under the aegis of the Faculty of Engineering.

8 Executive Master's in Business Administration.

9 Data from the 2001 Census quoted in the "Fact Sheet - Education", on the website of Indian and Northern Affairs Canada, http://www.ainc-inac.gc.ca downloaded October 18, 2007

10 Martin Kenney and Rafiq Dossani, "Offshoring and the future of US engineering: An overview," *The BRIDGE*, pub. by the US National Academy of Engineering, Fall 2005, pages 5–12.

Glossary

Basic research: research whose goal is only discovery, or seeking the answers to important unanswered questions about nature, about humans, and about humans in nature; basic research is generally organized as a program of investigation which can change as discoveries are made along the way.

Commercialization: the process of bringing a product (good or service) to market to create wealth

Creativity: the ability to look at something that others have been looking at and to see something new, and then to make that new perception apparent to others—creativity is expressed in the arts and letters, in design, in research …

Design: the creative process of solving the problem of meeting a specified human need under a set of constraints, such as a limit on cost, compatibility with existing systems, safety regulations, ergonomic requirements, etc. The output of design is a proposed realization of an artifact or system, its functioning, its structure, and its physical form. Its quality is measured by its functionality in meeting the need, and by attributes such as reliability, convenience in use, and esthetic appeal.

Development: the activities required to turn an idea or an invention into a product ready to be sold and used; design and testing are always involved.

Engineering: the professional activity of creating artifacts and systems to meet people's material needs, with **design** as the central process, **scientific knowledge** and **economic** considerations as its essential inputs, and public safety as its overriding responsibility.

Innovation: a generic term describing the two-part process of **having an idea** and **putting it into action,** or the result of that process. In our context, it's the process of creating a new product and bringing it to market. In that case, the idea takes the form of an **invention** and putting it into action is **commercialization.**

i.e., innovation = invention + commercialization

Invention: an idea conceived to meet a need together with the practical means by which it can be implemented.

Project research: research done to help solve a specified practical problem, often encountered in industry, that cannot be solved with existing knowledge; the research is organized as a project, with a schedule, a budget, a management structure, progress reports, etc.

R&D: the acronym for research and development, two closely related but very different activities; a label that aggregates them, often used in statistical reports and in policy documents.

Research: the process of learning what is not yet known by anyone, anywhere.

Science: the social system for creating new knowledge that involves three sequential and interrelated activities: **research** conducted according to the scientific method, **debate** to determine which results of research should be accepted as fact, and finally **predictions** based on facts. **Science** can also be used to denote the accumulation of scientific facts in a certain field.

Technology: the set of materials, tools and procedures that **predictably and reproducibly** combine to produce a specified desired effect in the material environment.

Appendix

| | Pop. (2005) | population structure | | | median age, yrs. | ratio of the labour force to population | area, sq.km. |
		0-14, %	15-64, %	65+, %			
US	295,734,000	20.6	67.0	12.4	36.27	0.505	9,631,418
China	1,306,314,000	21.4	71.0	7.60	32.26	0.606	9,596,960
Japan	127,417,000	14.3	66.2	19.5	42.64	0.521	377,835
India	1,080,264,000	31.2	63.9	4.90	24.66	0.460	3,287,590
Germany	82,431,000	14.4	66.7	18.9	42.16	0.526	357,021
UK	60,441,000	17.7	66.5	15.8	38.99	0.498	244,820
France	60,656,000	18.4	65.2	16.4	38.85	0.457	547,030
Italy	58,103,000	13.9	66.7	19.4	41.77	0.421	301,230
Brazil	186,113,000	26.1	67.9	6.00	27.81	0.486	8,511,965
Russia	143,420,000	14.6	71.3	14.2	38.15	0.518	17,075,200
Canada	32,805,000	17.9	68.9	13.2	38.54	0.529	9,984,670
Mexico	106,203,000	31.1	63.3	5.60	24.93	0.352	1,972,550
Spain	40,341,000	14.4	68.0	17.6	39.51	0.512	504,782
S. Korea	48,423,000	19.4	72.0	8.60	34.51	0.488	98,480
Australia	20,090,000	19.8	67.2	12.9	36.56	0.519	7,686,850
Taiwan	22,894,000	19.7	70.7	9.60	34.14	0.450	35,980
Netherlands	16,407,000	18.1	67.8	14.1	39.04	0.459	41,526
Sweden	9,002,000	17.1	65.5	17.4	40.60	0.499	449,964
Switzerland	7,489,000	16.6	68.0	15.4	39.77	0.507	41,290
Norway	4,593,000	19.5	65.7	14.8	38.17	0.523	324,220
Finland	5,223,000	17.3	66.8	15.9	40.97	0.500	338,145
Israel	6,277,000	26.5	63.7	9.80	29.39	0.386	20,770
Ireland	4,016,000	20.9	67.5	11.5	33.70	0.506	70,280
median values		18.4	67.0	14.1	38.17	0.500	

Appendix (continued)

	population density pers./sq.km.	arable land sq.km	arable land loading pers./sq.km.	area of water sq.km.	coastline km.	GDP (2005) trillion $ (PPP)	GDP/cap $(PPP)/cap
US	30.71	1752676	169	469495	19,924	12.37	41828
China	136.12	1436267	910	270550	14,500	8.158	6245
Japan	337.23	45681	2789	3091	29,751	3.867	30349
India	328.59	1617415	668	314400	7,000	3.678	3405
Germany	230.89	118212	697	7798	2,389	2.446	29673
UK	246.88	56677	1066	3230	12,429	1.867	30890
France	110.88	182950	332	1400	3,427	1.816	29939
Italy	192.89	81708	711	7210	7,600	1.645	28312
Brazil	21.86	588573	316	55455	7,491	1.58	8489
Russia	8.40	1245792	115	79400	37,653	1.535	10703
Canada	3.29	451038	73	891163	202,080	1.077	32830
Mexico	53.84	249802	425	49510	9,330	1.066	10037
Spain	79.92	130231	310	5240	4,946	1.014	25136
S. Korea	491.70	16869	2871	290	2,413	0.9833	20306
Australia	2.61	498974	40	68290	25,760	0.6427	31991
Taiwan	636.30	7742	2957	3720	1,566	0.6108	26679
Netherlands	395.10	9050	1813	7643	451	0.5	30475
Sweden	20.01	26875	335	39030	3,218	0.2665	29605
Switzerland	181.38	4144	1807	1520	0	0.2621	34998
Norway	14.17	8836	520	16360	25,148	0.1947	42391
Finland	15.45	21891	239	33672	1,250	0.1584	30327
Israel	302.21	3332	1884	440	273	0.1392	22176
Ireland	57.14	26560	151	1390	1,448	0.1369	34089
median values	110.88		520		7000		29673

Appendix *(continued)*

	GDP composition			electricity consumption billion kWh/yr	elec. consum. per capita kWh/cap.yr.	oil consum. million bbl/day	oil consum. per capita bbl/day cap.
	agricult.%	industry %	services %				
US	1.0	20.7	78.3	3656	12362	20.030	0.0677
China	14.4	53.1	32.5	2170	1661	6.390	0.0049
Japan	1.3	25.3	73.5	946.3	7427	5.580	0.0438
India	20.6	28.1	51.4	519	480	2.320	0.0021
Germany	1.1	28.6	70.3	510.4	6192	2.680	0.0325
UK	1.1	26.0	72.9	346.1	5726	1.720	0.0285
France	2.5	21.4	76.1	433.3	7144	2.060	0.0340
Italy	2.1	28.8	69.1	302.2	5201	1.874	0.0323
Brazil	20.0	14.0	66.0	371.4	1996	2.100	0.0113
Russia	5.0	35.0	60.0	811.5	5658	2.800	0.0195
Canada	2.2	29.1	68.7	520.9	15879	2.193	0.0668
Mexico	18.0	24.0	58.0	193.9	1826	1.752	0.0165
Spain	3.4	28.7	67.9	231.1	5731	1.544	0.0383
S. Korea	3.8	41.4	54.8	303.3	6264	2.168	0.0448
Australia	4.0	26.4	69.6	200.7	9990	0.876	0.0436
Taiwan	1.6	29.3	69.0	206.1	9002	0.915	0.0400
Netherlands	2.1	24.4	73.5	101.6	6192	0.920	0.0561
Sweden	1.8	28.6	69.7	131.8	14641	0.346	0.0384
Switzerland	1.5	34.0	64.5	55.9	7464	0.259	0.0346
Norway	2.2	37.2	60.6	106.1	23100	0.257	0.0560
Finland	3.1	30.4	66.5	78.9	15106	0.220	0.0421
Israel	2.8	37.7	59.5	39.7	6325	0.270	0.0430
Ireland	5.0	46.0	49.0	23	5727	0.176	0.0438
median values	2.5	28.7	67.9		6264		0.0384

Appendix *(continued)*

	telecommunications		land lines per capita no./cap.	mobiles per capita no./cap.	land lines and mobiles per capita no./cap	roads	
	land lines millions	mobile millions				paved 000 km	unpaved 000 km
US	181.60	158.70	0.614	0.537	1.151	4180.00	2214.0
China	263.00	269.00	0.201	0.206	0.407	1448.00	362.0
Japan	71.15	86.66	0.558	0.680	1.239	914.70	262.5
India	48.90	26.15	0.045	0.024	0.069	3851.00	1440.0
Germany	54.35	64.80	0.659	0.786	1.445	231.60	0.0
UK	34.90	49.68	0.577	0.822	1.399	392.90	0.0
France	33.90	41.68	0.559	0.687	1.246	891.30	0.0
Italy	26.60	55.92	0.458	0.962	1.420	479.70	0.0
Brazil	38.81	46.37	0.209	0.249	0.458	94.87	1630.0
Russia	35.50	17.61	0.248	0.123	0.370	362.10	175.2
Canada	19.95	13.22	0.608	0.403	1.011	493.10	915.7
Mexico	15.96	28.13	0.150	0.265	0.415	108.10	221.4
Spain	17.57	37.51	0.436	0.930	1.365	658.20	6.7
S. Korea	22.88	33.59	0.473	0.694	1.166	74.64	22.6
Australia	10.81	14.35	0.538	0.714	1.252	316.50	495.1
Taiwan	13.36	25.09	0.584	1.096	1.679	37.30	1.7
Netherlands	10.00	12.50	0.609	0.762	1.371	104.80	11.7
Sweden	6.58	7.95	0.731	0.883	1.614	167.60	45.6
Switzerland	5.42	6.17	0.724	0.824	1.548	71.20	0.0
Norway	3.34	4.16	0.727	0.906	1.633	71.20	20.7
Finland	2.55	4.70	0.488	0.900	1.388	50.60	27.6
Israel	3.00	6.33	0.478	1.008	1.486	17.20	0.0
Ireland	1.96	3.40	0.488	0.847	1.335	95.70	0.0
median values			0.538	0.762	1.335		

Appendix *(continued)*

	expressw 000 km	airport paved no.	railways 000 km	ports no.
US	74.40	5120	227.736	24
China	29.70	389	71.898	7
Japan	6.95	142	23.577	10
India	n/a	239	63.230	8
Germany	12.04	332	46.142	10
UK	3.43	334	17.274	8
France	10.39	288	29.519	10
Italy	6.62	98	19.319	8
Brazil	0.00	709	29.412	9
Russia	0.00	640	87.157	10
Canada	16.91	508	48.683	9
Mexico	6.43	227	17.634	7
Spain	11.15	95	14.781	8
S. Korea	2.78	70	3.472	5
Australia	n/a	308	54.439	11
Taiwan	n/a	38	2.497	5
Netherlands	2.24	20	2.808	7
Sweden	1.54	155	11.481	9
Switzerland	1.71	42	4.257	0
Norway	0.18	67	4.077	8
Finland	0.65	76	5.851	10
Israel	0.13	28	0.640	4
Ireland	0.13	15	3.312	5

Index

Printed and bound in January 2008
by TRI-GRAPHIC PRINTING, Ottawa, Ontario,
for THE UNIVERSITY OF OTTAWA PRESS

Typeset in 10.5 on 12 Minion
by Ghislain Viau, CREATIVE PUBLISHING BOOK DESIGN

Copy-edited by Richard Thompson
Proofread by Lyne St-Hilaire-Tardif
Cover designed by CATHY MACLEAN DESIGN

Printed on TG Eco 100